796.510NE

100 Walks in
Lancashire

BT 0231586 6

BOLTON LIBRARIES

D1337842

231586 6

100 WALKS IN
Lancashire

compiled by

C HARLIE E METT

The Crowood Press

First published in 1992 by
The Crowood Press Ltd
Ramsbury
Marlborough
Wiltshire SN8 2HR

Revised edition 1995

British Library Cataloguing-in-Publication Data
A catalogue record for this book is
available from the British Library

ISBN 1 85223 892 5

Maps by Sharon Perks and Janet Powell

Typeset by Carreg Limited, Ross-on-Wye, Herefordshire

Printed by Redwood Books, Trowbridge, Wiltshire

Contents

1	Stanah and Cockles Hall	$^3/_4$m	(1km)
2	The Longton Meres	1m	($1^1/_2$km)
3	Beacon Fell Country Park	$1^1/_2$m	($2^1/_2$km)
4	Withnell	$1^1/_2$m	($2^1/_2$km)
5	Calder Vale	$1^1/_2$m	($2^1/_2$km)
6	Lowgill and Over Houses Great Wood	2m	(3km)
7	Wray and Hornby Castle	2m	(3km)
8	Mellor Brook	2m	(3km)
9	Churchtown	2m	(3km)
10	… and longer version	$8^1/_2$m	($13^1/_2$km)
11	Great Eccleston, Cartford Toll Bridge	2m	(3km)
12	The River Wyre at Garstang	2m	(3km)
13	The Drumlin	2m	(3km)
14	Slaidburn and Higher High Field	$2^1/_2$m	(4km)
15	Russels Farm	$2^1/_2$m	(4km)
16	Crossgill and Littledale Hall	$2^1/_2$m	(4km)
17	Blake Hall	$2^1/_2$m	(4km)
18	Barker Brow and White Holme	$2^1/_2$m	(4km)
19	Copster Green and Harwood Fold	$2^1/_2$m	(4km)
20	Abbey Village and Millstone Edge	$2^1/_2$m	(4km)
21	Park Bridge and Copy Nook Farm	3m	(5km)
22	Ryal Fold and Jubilee Tower	3m	(5km)
23	Grindleton and Foxley Bank	3m	(5km)
24	Slaidburn and Shay House	3m	(5km)
25	Wray	3m	(5km)
26	Feniscowles Paper Mills	3m	(5km)
27	Calder Vale	3m	(5km)
28	Skippool and Little Thornton	3m	(5km)
29	Where Wenning and Lune Meet	3m	(5km)
30	Denny Beck and Crook o' Lune	3m	(5km)
31	Solomon's Temple	3m	(5km)
32	Silverdale, Heald Brow and Woodwell	$3^1/_2$m	($5^1/_2$km)
33	Hoghton Tower	$3^1/_2$m	($5^1/_2$km)
34	Darwen Moor	$3^1/_2$m	($5^1/_2$km)

35	Higher Stony Bank	3½m	(5½km)
36	Samlesbury	3½m	(5½km)
37	Thornton Lodge and Cockle Hall	3½m	(5½km)
38	Blacko and Alkincoats	4m	(6½km)
39	Chipping and Loud Mytham	4m	(6½km)
40	Lady Hamilton's Well	4m	(6½km)
41	Leighton Moss	4m	(6½km)
42	Carnforth and Bolton-le-Sands	4m	(6½km)
43	Wycoller Country Park	4m	(6½km)
44	Stanah to Skippool	4m	(6½km)
45	... and longer version	8m	(13km)
46	Knott End-on-Sea	4m	(6½km)
47	... and longer version	8m	(13km)
48	Blacko and the Pasture House	4½m	(7km)
49	Plain Quarry and Hutton Roof Crags	4½m	(7km)
50	Salterforth and Daubers	4½m	(7km)
51	Freckleton and The Naze	4½m	(7km)
52	Newton and Slaidburn	4½m	(7km)
53	Conder Green and Old Glasson	4½m	(7km)
54	Fluke Hall, Bourbles, Tongues Lane	4½m	(7km)
55	Deerplay to Rising Bridge	5m	(8km)
56	... and longer version	8½m	(13½km)
57	Rising Bridge to Clough Head	5m	(8km)
58	... and longer version	13½m	(21½km)
59	Arnside and Arnside Knott	5m	(8km)
60	Whitewell and Crimpton	5m	(8km)
61	West Bradford and Grindleton	5m	(8km)
62	Newton and Rough Syke Barn	5m	(8km)
63	Withnell Fold Nature Reserve	5m	(8km)
64	The Lancaster Canal at Brock	5m	(8km)
65	Marles Wood and Copster Green	5m	(8km)
66	Overton and Sunderland Point	5m	(8km)
67	Longton and Walmer Bridge	5m	(8km)
68	Hornby and Gressingham	5m	(8km)
69	Garstang	5m	(8km)
70	... and longer version	6m	(9½km)

71	Kirkham, Wesham and Wrea Green	5$^1/_2$m	(9km)
72	Yealand Storrs and Leighton Moss	5$^1/_2$m	(9km)
73	Fairy Steps and Haverbrack	5$^1/_2$m	(9km)
74	Kelbrook and Harden Clough	5$^1/_2$m	(9km)
75	Kelbrook and Black Lane Ends	5$^1/_2$m	(9km)
76	Earby and Kelbrook Circular	5$^1/_2$m	(9km)
77	Tockholes	5$^1/_2$m	(9km)
78	West Bradford and Foxley Bank	5$^1/_2$m	(9km)
79	Lytham Lifeboat Station	6m	(9$^1/_2$km)
80	Bacup, Sharneyford and Deerplay	6m	(9$^1/_2$km)
81	Barnoldswick and Weets Hill	6m	(9$^1/_2$km)
82	Hoghton Gorge Circular	6m	(9$^1/_2$km)
83	The Warland Reservoirs	6m	(9$^1/_2$km)
84	Riverside Park	6m	(9$^1/_2$km)
85	… and longer version	12m	(19km)
86	Healey Dell to Sharneyford	6$^1/_2$m	(10$^1/_2$km)
87	Blacko and Foulridge	6$^1/_2$m	(10$^1/_2$km)
88	Trawden and Coldwell	6$^1/_2$m	(10$^1/_2$km)
89	Brierfield to Wheatley Lane Circular	7m	(11km)
90	Stubbins to Healey Dell	7m	(11km)
91	… and longer version	14$^1/_2$m	(23km)
92	Garstang and the Lancaster Canal	7m	(11km)
93	Fleetwood and Stanah	7m	(11km)
94	Winmarleigh Moss	7$^1/_2$m	(12km)
95	Borwick and Warton	8$^1/_4$m	(13km)
96	Greenber Field and Barnoldswick	9m	(14$^1/_2$km)
97	Barrowford and Slipper Hill	9m	(14$^1/_2$km)
98	Ribchester and Stonyhurst	9m	(14$^1/_2$km)
99	Ribchester and Bolton Fold Cross	9m	(14$^1/_2$km)
100	Blackpool's Golden Mile	12m	(19km)

PUBLISHER'S NOTE

We very much hope that you enjoy the routes presented in this book, which has been compiled with the aim of allowing you to explore the area in the best possible way - on foot.

We strongly recommend that you take the relevant map for the area, and for this reason we list the appropriate Ordnance Survey maps for each route. Whilst the details and descriptions given for each walk were accurate at time of writing, the countryside is constantly changing, and a map will be essential if, for any reason, you are unable to follow the given route. It is good practice to carry a map and use it so that you are always aware of your exact location.

We cannot be held responsible if some of the details in the route descriptions are found to be inaccurate, but should be grateful if walkers would advise us of any major alterations. Please note that whenever you are walking in the countryside you are on somebody else's land, and we must stress that you should *always* keep to established rights of way, and *never* cross fences, hedges or other boundaries unless there is a clear crossing point.

Remember the country code:

Enjoy the country and respect its life and work
Guard against all risk of fire
Fasten all gates
Keep dogs under close control
Keep to public footpaths across all farmland
Use gates and stiles to cross field boundaries
Leave all livestock, machinery and crops alone
Take your litter home
Help to keep all water clean
Protect wildlife, plants and trees
Make no unnecessary noise

The walks are listed by length - from approximately 1 to 12 miles - but the amount of time taken will depend on the fitness of the walkers and the time spent exploring any points of interest along the way. Nearly all the walks are circular and most offer recommendations for refreshments.

Good walking.

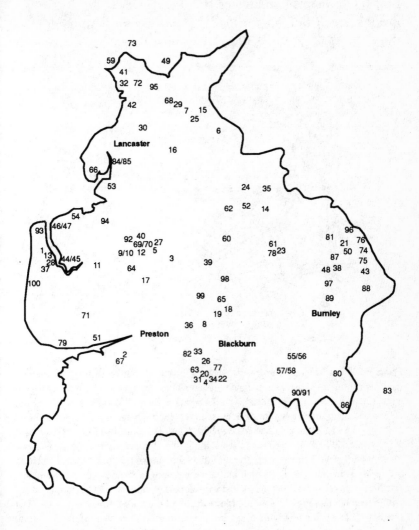

73

59
49
41
32 72 95
42
68 29 7 15
25
30
6
Lancaster
16
84/85
66
53
24 35
54
62 52 14
94
93 46/47
92 40 27
60
1 69/70
81 96
13 9/10 12 5
61 21 76
28 44/45 3
78 23 50 74
37 11
39
87 75
64
48 38 43
100
17
98
97 88
99
89
19 18 65
Burnley
71
36 8
79 51
Preston
Blackburn
2
82 33
67
26 77
55/56
63 20
57/58
31 4 34 22
80
83
90/91
86

Walk 1   STANAH AND COCKLES HALL $^3/_4$m (1km)

Maps: OS Sheets Landranger 102; Pathfinder 658.
A nature trail suitable for the blind and partially sighted.
Start: At 355432, Wyre Ecology Centre, Stanah.

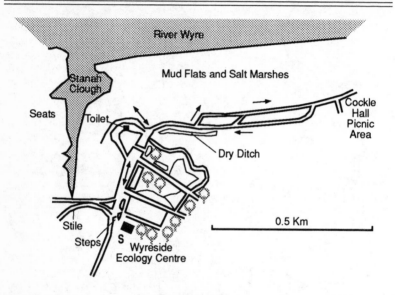

From the **Wyre Ecology Centre**, go forward, briefly, towards facing steps, turning right short of them along a tarmac path, passing a bus stop on the left. Where the path ends, turn left, passing a picnic area on the right, and turn first right, still edging the picnic area. Continue along the road, crossing a sleeping policeman. Follow the road as it curves to the right, at which point a short detour left to the right side of a car park is recommended. There, near some seats, a plinth and board give information about the Wyre estuary. Retrace your steps to the road and turn left, beside a dry ditch on the right. Turn left, down a slope and continue along a riverside path. The plants growing here are called halophites and are tolerant of salt water. The path is edged with a wooden tapping rail, looking like a skirting board, all the way to Cockle Hall picnic site. The rail enables the blind and the partially sighted to confidently follow the path either by tapping the rail, or running their stick along it. This simple, but very effective, way of sharing the joys of walking in the **Wyre estuary** is a most admirable innovation, one that other authorities would do well to follow.

The path continues through the trees, soon passing, on the right, a short path leading up the bank on the right, and, a little further on, a second path on the right, leading up the same bank. Between these two path junctions the lower path is not suitable for wheelchairs. From this second lateral path continue straight ahead to Cockle Hall picnic area. From it, retrace your steps to the first of the two short paths leading up the slope. Now turn right and continue along the bank top using a path that is admirably suited to the needs of wheelchair users. Keep going, parallel to and above the path used on the outward leg. Once past the slope used near the start of the walk, retrace your steps to the Ecology Centre.

POINTS OF INTEREST:

Wyre Ecology Centre – Access to the Centre is through double doors and inside there is a lower disabled counter and shelf containing information brochures. There is a toilet for the disabled at the rear of the building and ample parking space for the disabled at the front. Several of the picnic tables are suitable for wheelchair use and level surfaced paths thread the Country Park, many of which are suitable for people with wheelchairs or pushchairs. Facilities for the blind and partially sighted include the trail with its tapping rail. To accompany this, there is a self-guided tape which can be hired, together with the player, from the visitor centre.

Wyre estuary – Most of the local area rests on boulder clay overlying a mixture of mudstone and sandstone bedrock. In the mudstone, between Preesall and the estuary, are salt deposits, up to 600 feet (almost 185 metres) thick. These deposits led to the development of the local chemical industry. In 1892 the United Alkali Company mined rock salt at Preesall: in 1926 the Company was acquired by ICI. During World War II, ICI Hillhouse was started to produce various kinds of war chemicals, many chlorine based. With the loss of the Far East rubber plants, PVC production began at Hillhouse in 1944. The saltmines at Preesall have now been flooded: the brine is pumped out, across to the Hillhouse site, the pipe running through Stanah.

REFRESHMENTS:
Farm House Kitchen, Stanah.

Walk 2   THE LONGTON MERES   1m (1¹/₂km)

Maps: OS Sheets Landranger 102; Pathfinder 688.

A short walk specially designed for wheelchair bound people and those unable to walk very far.

Start: At 479251, the car park on the main road into Longton.

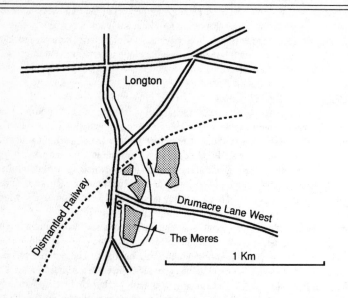

It is heartening to discover that such walks for the disabled exist. They are a most welcome addition to the walking scene and more would be welcome.

From the car park, a little to the south of the junction of Drumacre Lane, go eastwards towards the largest and nearest of the nearby meres. Continue around the mere on an elevated pathway, which is suitable for wheelchairs. On reaching the top right-hand corner of the mere continue northwards briefly, then cross a stile specially designed to accommodate a wheelchair and cross Drumacre Lane.

Keep straight ahead, going along the eastern side of another mere, on your left, which has, to the north of it, another tiny mere. Continue straight ahead, going to the left of the fourth mere. Just past it, turn left, over another stile, into Briarcroft, on the outskirts of **Longton**. Turn left again into School Lane and go along it, passing a modern housing development, Ashwood Court, on the left. Stay on School Lane, soon joining a path that goes diagonally right and through wrought iron gates on to the main road. Turn left, alongside it, for about 300 yards to return to the car park.

POINTS OF INTEREST:

Longton – Aeons ago, the countryside to the south of Preston was covered in forests, beech, juniper, hazel and willow at first, later replaced by oaks and other deciduous trees. But the forests did not dominate the entire early landscape, to the east, on the south side of the Ribble, the low lying land was ill-drained, and mosses and coarse grasses flourished. These grasslands provided feeding grounds for the animals on which early hunting man depended. About 6000 years ago, early man began to domesticate animals and grow cereal crops. This led to the development of separate farming communities: many of the scattered Fylde communities, such as Longton, came into being this way.

Sited in such a wet environment, the farming community of Longton was kept busy draining areas of wetland in order to increase the amount of wheat, oats and vegetables. Fruit and dairy products were also important to Longton's economy. Surplus produce was sent to the expanding town of Preston. Preston, the oldest borough in Lancashire and the administrative centre of the county, had developed as a market centre, meeting the needs of the region. Unlike Lancaster, it was not a dynastic stronghold with walls and a castle. It was dominated by its market, which had developed in response to local needs.

As Lancashire's cotton industry developed in the last decades of the 17th century, so Preston expanded. The town's first spinning mill was built around 1777, yet despite the increasing mechanisation of spinning, the late 18th century was the golden age of the handloom weavers, who worked at their own homes, controlled by putters-out, who supplied yarn and collected finished pieces. The handloom weavers, of whom, Longton had its share, provided sufficient cheap cloth to make further expansion of cloth exports possible. Much of the production was later centralised in warehouses, one of which was at Longton.

Today Preston is close to swallowing Longton which has become a dormitory suburb of the town.

REFRESHMENTS:

None on the route but in available in nearby Longton.

Walk 3   BEACON FELL COUNTRY PARK $1\frac{1}{2}$m ($2\frac{1}{2}$km)

Maps: OS Sheets Landranger 102; Pathfinder 668.
An isolated hill of rough moorland and mixed woodland.
Start: At 566424, Crombleholme car park.

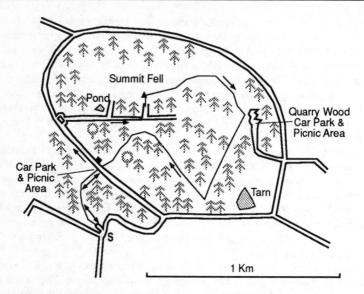

From the car park, at the southern edge of Beacon Fell Country Park, go westwards, away from the road, along a track which edges woodland on the right. Where the path forks, take the right-hand branch which climbs through conifers. Beyond, the path reaches Metcalf's car park and snack bar. Turn right, briefly, then turn left along a road that passes a toilet block. Soon two tracks, to the right, lead into the forest: take either as they soon meet at a signpost for 'Beacon Fell Country Park Fell Side Trail'. Continue along the broad track they form, going uphill through pines. Many paths criss-cross and all are exciting to explore. This route has been chosen because it covers most of the park and visits Beacon Hill's summit. Ignore all side tracks, going uphill through Dewpond Wood, passing the pond on the left. Just past it, continue ahead at a crossing of tracks, contouring for a short distance, then climbing slightly to reach another track that is followed to the trig. point summit of **Beacon Hill** seen ahead.

12

At the trig. point, face north, then turn right along a broad track through rough, heather-clad moorland. Soon, descend steps and contour through open country. The track leads to more steps down to a surfaced parking area. Do not descend these steps: instead, turn right, staying on the track and climbing slightly at first, then contouring. Go past a lovely **tarn**, a little to the left and lower down. The track now has a surface of bark chips: it cuts through conifers, with several paths leading from it to the tarn. Where another track joins from the left, simply keep ahead, soon bearing slightly right and climbing through an avenue of larches. The track then begins to descend through mixed woodland. On reaching a T-junction, turn along another track, going through more conifers. Where the track climbs out of woodland, continue over the brow of the hillside and bear left, passing the entrance to Queens Grove Path on the right. Now descend to Metcalf's car park, which you passed through on the outward leg. From it, retrace your steps back to the start.

POINTS OF INTEREST:
Beacon Hill – A beacon once stood on the 873 foot (266m) summit where the triangulation pillar is sited, one of a chain used to warn of impending danger like the approach of the Spanish Armada in 1588. The beacon was probably a pitch barrel which was fired at night and smoked during the day. From the summit, a magnificent viewpoint, looking left to right, you can see, on a clear day, the North Wales mountains, the Isle of Man, the Lakeland fells, the Bowland fells and Pendle Hill. Spread before you is north-west Lancashire, its most famous symbol, Blackpool Tower, and the new roller coaster, the tallest in the world, can be clearly seen.

Tarn – Created to provide a source of water for fire-fighting the tarn is now a valuable wildlife area. The walk also passes other valuable wildlife sites. The woodland, moorland, farmland and wet areas provide important habitats for a variety of flora and fauna. Skylark, meadow-pipit, curlew and lapwing are all found on the moorland and surrounding farmland. Within the woodland there are tits, chaffinch, willow warbler, goldcrest, bullfinch, siskin and crossbill.

REFRESHMENTS:
Metcalf's Car Park Snack Bar. There are also several picnic sites in the Park.

Maps: OS Sheets Landranger 103; Pathfinder 689.
A gentle field walk through a pleasing countryside.
Start: At 631224, St Paul's Church, Withnell.

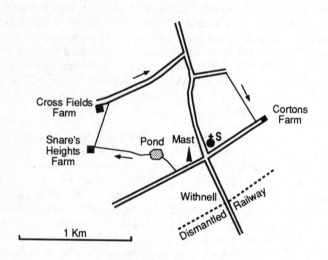

Turn left from the church and, at the end of the churchyard, cross a road and turn right, up a lane. Just past the gable end of a row of houses on the left, go through a wicket to the left of a gate and continue along the lane. Across the valley to the left from here, the huge gash of Brinscall quarry slices the moorland. When the track forks, take the left branch, going ahead, with a tall mast to the right. Where the track goes between a pair of gate posts, turn right and walk along the hedge on your right. When the hedge ends, walk parallel to a section of broken wall on the right to reach a pond. Beyond, walk beside a hedge to reach stile in it. Go over and turn half-left across the rough pasture beyond, aiming for the left-hand corner of a wood. Go over a stile and edge the next field close to the wood, on your right. The gable end seen ahead belongs to Snape's Heights Farm. Just short of the field's right-hand corner, turn right over a stile and cross the field beyond, staying close to, at first, a wall on the left, then a mix of hawthorns and fencing. Go over a stile close to the left-hand corner of the field, and go diagonally right across a field to reach a stile by a gate to the right of a hedge of conifers. Go along a green lane, passing to the right of Cross Fields Farm.

Soon, go over a stile to the left of a gate on to the farm's access road, and turn right along it. At the road end, cross the facing road and turn right along it. As it curves right, turn left along a gated farm lane, as directed by a footpath sign. At the farm, where the road turns right, go ahead, along the right-hand side of a hawthorn hedge. After a few yards, turn left, over a stile, then turn right along a concrete road. Where this curves to the right, go right, on the bend, over a stile and continue straight across the field, close to the hedge on the right. Go over a stile in the right-hand corner, walk forward for a few yards, then turn right along a concrete road. Soon, go through a gateway and turn left over a step stile. Cross the field beyond, staying close to the fence on your left and go through a gate on to a track that leads to Gorton's Farm on your left. Turn right, along the track, and cross a stile to the left of a gate that marks the farm entrance. A few yards ahead is St Paul's Church, **Withnell**: continue with it on your left, and on reaching its front, right-hand, corner turn left along the footpath, briefly, to reach the entrance.

POINTS OF INTEREST:
Withnell – The village lies in the rural part of Lancashire, a county which is predominantly industrial. By the time of Queen Victoria's Silver Jubilee only six per cent of the population were involved with farming. Even part-time farmers like those who also worked as hand loom weavers were decreasing. During the early years of the 19th century, long horned cattle were bred in large numbers, but by the middle of that century they had been replaced, for the most part, by short horns. Today Friesians have become the most popular breed on north Lancashire cattle breeding farms and many dairy farms are supplemented by egg and poultry productions.

REFRESHMENTS:
Sorry! none on this one. Please bring your own.

Walk 5   CALDER VALE $1\frac{1}{2}$m ($2\frac{1}{2}$km)

Maps: OS Sheets Landranger 102; Pathfinder 668.

Milling around Calder Vale's mills!

Start: At 532457, the northern end of Albert Terrace, Calder Vale.

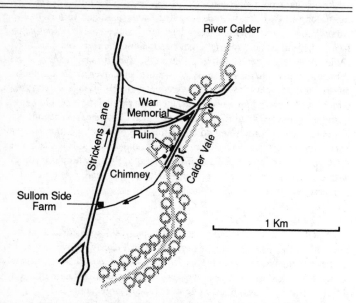

From the point on the minor road, that climbs through Calder Village, where Albert Terrace leads away from it, go along the Terrace, passing cottages on your left. In less than 400 yards, the last of the cottages is passed and the way continues straight ahead along a broad, clear track that cuts though a wooded bank, parallel to and above the River Calder. Continue past, and above, the lodge of a demolished mill and cross a feeder on footbridges to reach some cottages and the house of the owner of the, now demolished, **Barnacre Mill**.

Go past the cottages and a barrier, and when the track curves left, leave it to follow a climbing track that shoots off to the right. Go through woodland to reach a facing gate. Go through into a field and cross it, staying close to the fence on the left. Exit through a facing gate at an obtuse field corner and continue along a climbing lane that passes to the left of Sullom Side Farm to reach Strickens Lane. Turn right along the lane to pass, after about $\frac{1}{2}$ mile, a road junction on the right. Continue to reach, a $\frac{1}{3}$ of a mile further on, a bungalow on the right, close to where there are three gates. Go through the middle gate and diagonally right, edging a field close to the fence on the right. Leave the field over a stile at a footpath sign and continue alongside a ditch, with bungalows behind it, to leave the field over a stile in the field corner. Turn left, go over a footbridge and cross the field beyond, leaving over a facing stile a little to the right of a telegraph pole. Keep straight ahead, walking parallel to some buildings over on the right. Leave the field over a facing stile and continue along a lane that edges a small wood on the left. Now walk alongside houses on the right to reach some steps. Go down these to reach the road that descends through **Calder Vale**. Turn right along it, briefly, to reach Albert Terrace where the walk began.

POINTS OF INTEREST:

Barnacre Mill – In 1845, the Barnacre weaving mill was opened. It was powered by a waterwheel fed by water piped over the entrance arch. Later, a steam engine provided the power. The steam engine's chimney was built on the ground above the woodland that edges the River Calder.

Slightly downstream of the Barnacre mill, just past the cottages, there was once a single storey mill.

Calder Vale – Sited in a fold of the Bowland foothills, Calder Vale is a stone-built industrial village. In 1835 a four-storey cotton mill was built here, and the remains of the old mill race can still be seen above the village. At first a waterwheel produced the power: a turbine replaced it, and a beam engine replaced that, only to be replaced, in turn, by a gas engine in 1909. Today the mill's is powered by electricity: the mill exports head dresses to the Arabs. The Jackson family built the mill and the village to house the Mill's employees. The family, all Quakers, did not wish to see children of Calder Vale dressed in rags, as had happened in so many other centres of industry at that time, so they did not encourage drink which was thought to be the main cause of country's penury. Consequently, Calder Vale has no pub.

REFRESHMENTS:

As mentioned above, there is no pub in Calder Vale, so please bring your own refreshments.

Walk 6 LOWGILL AND OVER HOUSES GREAT WOOD 2m (3km)
Maps: OS Sheets Landranger 97; Pathfinder 650.
A pleasant field walk with a double crossing of the River Hindburn.
Start: At 653648, the Methodist Church, Lowgill.

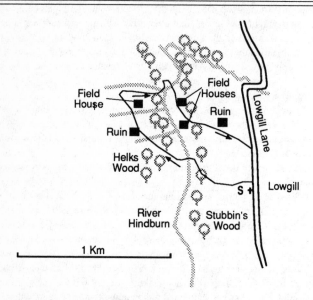

From the church turn left and almost at once turn left again, through a metal gate. Bear left along a track to reach a facing gate. Go through and walk down the field beyond on the clear track close to the wall on the left. Where the wall ends, keep straight ahead, leaving the field over a stile to the left of a facing gate. Now go forward, down a long narrow field, descending gently.

Exit the field over a stile, to the right of a metal gate, into woodland and immediately turn left along a clear path which soon descends quite steeply and curves to the right. At the bottom of the bank, leave the wood through a gap stile. Go diagonally right across the field beyond to a reach a footbridge over the River Hindburn. Cross and immediately cross a stile and climb some steps. At the top, continue straight ahead over undulating rough pasture up the valley side, bearing slightly left to climb up a clear depression to the left of a line of telegraph poles. When the land levels, and what remains of a facing wall is reached, bear to the right, along another depression, going between bracken to reach a facing gate.

Continue climbing along the depression, going between trees, and, on reaching its head, cross the field ahead to go over a brook that flows down at a point between a silver birch, on the left, and an alder. Keep straight ahead, walking parallel to the wall on the left, and in a short distance a gate is seen in a facing fence. Go through and continue ahead, crossing a field to reach a facing gate, passing, on the left, a ruinous building. Go through the gate and maintain direction across the next field. Exit through a gate to the left of a building. Cross the next field diagonally left to reach its left-hand corner. There, turn right and edge the gill on your left. Exit the field over a stile, into woodland, in the left-hand corner of a facing wall. Follow a path through the trees, bearing right as you descend a bank.

The **River Hindburn** is at the foot of the bank, but the path curves left, leaving the wood over a step stile in the fence on the left. Follow the path ahead, walking parallel to the river, on the right. Within a short distance the path reaches a footbridge over the river. Cross and go straight over the field beyond, aiming for the right-hand side of a protruding wooded bank, not the end of the field. On reaching the bank continue along its foot, soon passing a building on the left. Leave the field over a stile in a facing wall, some distance to the left of a gate.

Continue across the next field, still walking along the bottom of the wooded bank on the left, to a point where, just past a field house on the right, you go left along a path that climbs the wooded bank. Go over a stile in a facing section of wall and head diagonally right over the field beyond to reach its right-hand corner. As a guide there is a ruinous building on the left. Go over a stile to the left of a gate and continue diagonally right to reach the right-hand corner of the large field beyond. Go through a gate into Lowgill Lane. Turn right along the lane to regain the start.

POINTS OF INTEREST:
River Hindburn – This beautiful river is especially attractive in the area of this walk.

REFRESHMENTS:
Sorry, none on the route – you must bring your own!

Walk 7   **WRAY AND HORNBY CASTLE**   2m (3km)

Maps: OS Sheets Landranger 97; Pathfinder 637.

Where the Eagle Tower of Hornby Castle soars in romantic splendour above the River Wenning.

Start: At 602677, the Methodist Chapel, Wray.

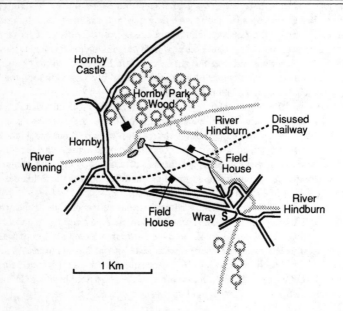

From the chapel go diagonally left across the road and continue along Kiln Lane. Where the lane splits into three, take the left fork, from where there are good views of **Hornby Castle** ahead, to the right. Soon a gate is reached on the right. Go through this, and a second further on, and go diagonally left across a field aiming to the right of a building at the far side. Exit through a gate in the fence on the left, just beyond the building. Go diagonally right across the corner of the next field to reach a disused railway line. Turn left, along it, soon reaching two concrete wickets, one each side. Turn right here and go over a stile into a field. Cross the field, bearing slightly right to reach a gate at its right-hand corner. Go through and cross the next field close to the

20

hedge/fence on the right with Hornby Castle ahead. Go through a gate in the fence on the right and go diagonally right across the field beyond to a gate in a hawthorn hedge.

Go diagonally right across the next field to reach a fence. Go through the right-hand of two gates in it and walk straight across the field beyond to reach a gate in a wall. Now go diagonally right across a field which has a field house near its left-hand corner, and leave through a wicket on to the disused railway track. Cross this, go through a gate and continue along a lane. At its end, at the River Hindburn, turn right through a gate into a field and cross it close to the fence on your left, with the river behind it. Leave the field through a gate and edge the next field close to the riverbank, following a field track which soon curves right, away from the river, to reach the point where you turned left on the outward leg. From here continue straight ahead, along the lane, back to the Methodist Chapel.

POINTS OF INTEREST:
Hornby Castle – Situated on a hill, this castle was built by the Normans. The gargoyles on its battlements were added by Sir Edward Stanley who commanded a contingent of Lancashire men-at-arms at the Battle of Flodden in 1513. A grateful King Henry VIII acknowledged Sir Edward's part in the defeat of the Scots by creating him Lord Monteagle. In return Lord Monteagle built the imposing Eagle Tower over the castle's central keep. Lord Monteagle also erected the eight-sided tower at the west end of St Margaret's Church in Hornby village. The castle later passed into the hands of Colonel Charteris, a notorious forger and gambler. The colonel was cashiered from the army for cheating at cards, and in 1713 he bought Hornby Castle with his gambling winnings.

REFRESHMENTS:
The New Inn, Wray.
The George and Dragon, Wray.

Walk 8   **MELLOR BROOK**   2m (3km)

Maps: OS Sheets Landranger 102; Pathfinder 680.

A haunting little walk, and a walk with a little haunting.

Start: At 639306, a road junction in Mellor Brook.

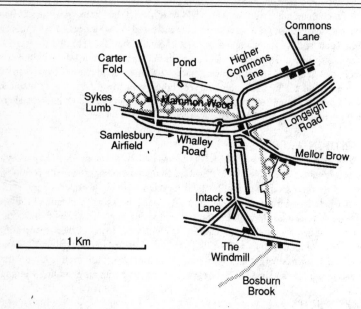

From the northern end of Intack Lane, where it joins Branch Road, cross the latter and go along a lane between houses, continuing through a wooded area to reach a stile. Go over and follow a path which descends towards Bosburn Brook. Before the Brook is reached, turn left along a path with the brook on the right. Cross a concrete bridge over the brook and immediately go over a stile. Continue along a path which follows the wooded left-hand side of the field, then pulls away from the trees on the left to follow trees on the right. Follow the path to a stile in the right-hand corner of the field. Cross the stile and follow a path between bungalows. At its end, turn right for a few yards, then left to reach a road, Mellor Brow.

Turn left along the road, descending into Mellor Brook. On reaching a point opposite 'Fir Trees' turn right, along an alley between houses. Cross Longsight Road and walk ahead down Higher Commons Lane. The lane goes under a bridge that carries a by-pass road, then crosses a bridge over Mellor Brook, as Bosburn Brook is now called. The lane continues into Mammon Wood, then curves right and climbs. At the brow of the hill leave the lane by turning left over a signed stile. Cross the field beyond, staying close to the fence on the left and exiting over a stile in the left-hand corner of a facing hedge. Cross the next field to reach a stile in the facing hedge. Go over and cross the next field, a long one, close to the hedge on your left. Where this hedge ends at a pond, skirt the pond and maintain direction across the field, bearing slightly right to reach a stile. Go over on to the old carriage drive to Balderstone Grange. Turn left along it, and as you do so, the buildings of Samlesbury airfield are seen on the right.

Go through a kissing gate, to the left of a larger gate, into Mammon Wood. Follow the carriage drive through the wood, soon passing Carter Fold on the right. Exit the wood by bridging Mellor Brook, close to the site of **Sykes Lumb**, then go over the by-pass, taking great care, and cross a signed stile. Continue along a broad track through a narrow wooded area, briefly, to reach Whalley Road. Turn left along it, using a roadside footpath, into **Mellor Brook** village. Turn right along Branch Road to return to the start of the walk.

POINTS OF INTEREST:

Sykes Lumb – During the 30 years of conflict between the houses of Lancaster and York (the Wars of the Roses) the Sykes family, who lived at Sykes Lumb, buried all their money for safety's sake. Sadly the couple died before they could recover it. Legend has it that Mrs Sykes' ghost was often seen trying to get the money. One evening a drunk followed her ghost to a spot in the orchard where she indicated, by pointing, where it was buried. The money, which had been buried in jars, was recovered and the ghost has not been seen since.

Mellor Brook – A spinning mill, complete with its pond, used to operate in the village and the end house of Victoria Terrace belonged to the mill's manager. Mill workers lived in the remaining houses of the terrace. The mill was demolished in 1924. 'Fir Trees', opposite where the route through the village turns right, used to be a Wesleyan Chapel.

REFRESHMENTS:

The Windmill Inn, Mellor Brook.
The Fieldens Arms, Mellor Brook.

Walks 9 & 10 **CHURCHTOWN** 2m (3km)
or 8¹/₂m (13¹/₂km)

Maps: OS Sheets Landranger 102; Pathfinder 668.
A gentle stroll through flat Fylde farmland.
Start: At 482428, St Helen's Church, Churchtown.

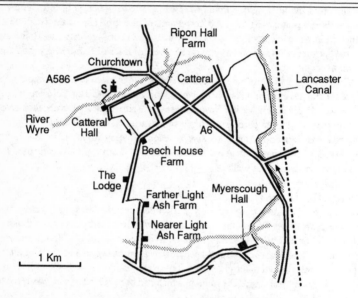

From the church's front gates, turn right, along a path through the churchyard. Go through a gate and walk across a field to cross a footbridge over the River Wyre. Cross a stile into a field. Soon, go through a gap stile and walk ahead to another into a lane. Follow the lane to its T-junction with Catterall Lane.

The shorter walk turns left here, passing several houses to reach the road to Ripon Hall Farm, on the left. The longer route rejoins here.

The longer walk turns right at the T-junction. Follow the lane to 'The Lodge'. There, go through a gate and along a green lane. Go over a stile and bear left along an embankment to another stile. Now follow the fence on the left towards Farther Light Ash Farm. Go to the right of the buildings to join the farm road. Follow this past Nearer Light Ash Farm. At the road end, turn left along a road, passing Myerscough

Lodge Farm on your right. Where the road bears right, turn left along the drive of Myerscough College. Take the first turn right, then go left at a T-junction, following a road through a gateway signed 'To the pavilion'. Follow the road to Bilsborough and the Lancaster Canal. Turn right, down steps, turn under the canal bridge and follow the towpath, with the canal on your right, for $2^1/_2$ miles. Just short of Catterall Basin, turn left along a lane to Sturzaker House Farm. Go between farm buildings and walk ahead to Catterall. Go over at a cross-roads to reach the A6. Cross, with care, and go along Catterall Lane to reach the road for Ripon Hall Farm, on the right. The shorter route is regained here.

Follow the farm road. At the farm, go between farm buildings, through a pair of gates, and, a few yards beyond, at another building, turn left to reach a gate into a field. Cross to a stile. Cross the next field to reach a ladder stile. Go over and turn left along a track. with the River Wyre on your right. Follow the track through three gates to reach the outward route. Turn right to retrace your steps back to **St Helen's Church**.

POINTS OF INTEREST:
St Helen's Church – Inside the church some very interesting wall paintings were discovered when plaster was removed in 1971. The paintings are of biblical texts in a decorative frame.

REFRESHMENTS:
The Punch Bowl Inn, Churchtown.

Walk 11 **GREAT ECCLESTON, CARTFORD TOLL BRIDGE** 2m (3km)
Maps: OS Sheets Landranger 102; Pathfinder 668.
A walking along the River Wyre's flood barrier.
Start: At 427401, the bus shelter opposite the White Bull Inn,
Great Eccleston.

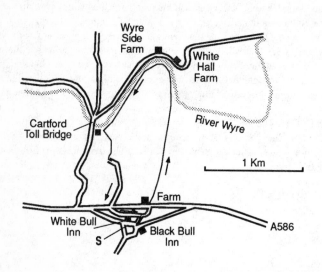

Go diagonally right across the road and down a side street, guided by a toilet sign on
a wall. At a T-junction by the entrance to business premises, turn right along a lane
and at its end turn left at a footpath sign. Go along a lane which soon turns right, then
left as a concrete lane. At its end, cross the busy A586, with care, bearing slightly
right to go through a gateway. Bear right over a signed stile and cross a field to reach
a stile in its bottom left-hand corner. Go over and cross a field close to a fence on the
right to reach a stile. Go over and climb on to an embankment, a flood barrier, and
turn left, with the **River Wyre** on the right. Go over a stile continuing along the
embankment to pass a farm on the right. On the far bank of the Wyre, just before the
river makes a bend to the left, is White Hall. As the river's curve begins, a footbridge
and an aqueduct, a pipe bridge, are passed. Pass Wyre Side Farm, on the river's far

bank, and go over a stile and continue to cross a step stile to the left of a gate. Where the river turns sharp right to go under Cartford Toll Bridge, and the embankment ends close to where, to the right, there is a car park, turn left, over a step stile, into a field. Go diagonally left to cross a footbridge over a ditch.

Go diagonally right across the next field to reach a stile in the right-hand corner. Go over and continue along Butt's Lane to reach the A586. Cross, with care, and continue along Butt's Lane, as directed by a footpath sign. Just past the gable end of a white painted house, turn left, along Back Lane. Where the lane reaches the same business premises, on the left, where you turned right on the outward leg, turn right to retrace your steps back to the start.

POINTS OF INTEREST:

River Wyre – Once the river has shaken itself free of the hill country of its birth, it enters an area of extensive mossland. It snakes its sluggish way along the southern side of Rawcliffe Moss where the land is so low lying that many local roads run along narrow embankments, several feet higher than the re-claimed land either side. Here confining embankments are used extensively to contain the Wyre which otherwise would flood, nullifying the draining work which began on the mosses in the 1830's. Draining and clearing the Over Wyre mosses was difficult work and regular maintenance is necessary to keep the drains and open ditches functioning efficiently. But the rewards have been splendid: the re-claimed land is excellent for both arable and dairy farming, potatoes and oats being the most popular crops.

REFRESHMENTS:
The White Bull Inn, Eccleston.
The Black Bull Inn, Eccleston.

Walk 12   THE RIVER WYRE AT GARSTANG   2m (3km)

Maps: OS Sheets Landranger 102; Pathfinder 668.

A pleasant way to round off a visit to Garstang.

Start: At 493454, the Community Centre car park, Garstang.

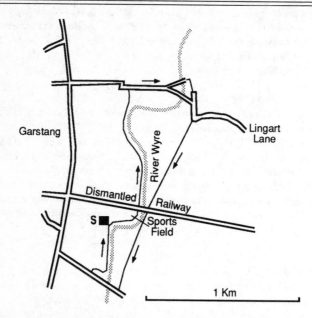

From the car park go left, briefly, to the River Wyre and turn left along a riverside footpath, heading upstream and edging a sportsfield on the left. On reaching a bridge that carries a dismantled railway over the river, go under it, climb the embankment ahead and descend to rejoin the riverside path. Continue upstream, soon crossing a small footbridge. Go over a stile a little further on, where the river bends. Continue close to the fence on the left to reach a stile on to a road. Turn right, but just past a double gate, go left, along a lane. Soon you reach the river: cross on a footbridge and turn right to edge a field. Go through a gate on to a lane.

Go along the lane to where it makes a sharp left turn. Now go over a facing stile and follow the right-hand boundary of the field beyond. Where this goes diagonally right, keep ahead to reach a stile. Go over and maintain direction, aiming to the right of a church tower with a spire. Go over a stile and maintain direction to reach another. Go over and climb on to the embankment of the **dismantled railway**. Bear right and descend to cross a stile on your left. Edge the next field along the riverbank on your right. Go over a stile and walk close to a fence on the left. Where this bends to the left, keep ahead, aiming for the left-hand side of a bridge over the Wyre. Go over a stile on to a road and turn right to cross the bridge. Go past some buildings on your right, but just past a bus garage, turn right along a track to the riverside. Now, with the River Wyre on your right, walk back to the car park in **Garstang**.

POINTS OF INTEREST:

Dismantled railway – The Garstang and Knott End Railway Act of 1864 authorised the building of this cross-mosses line. It was opened in 1870 from Garstang to Pilling; but it took 38 more years before the extension across the Wyre from Knott End to Fleetwood was opened. The people of Pilling were ecstatic, yet despite initial hopes that the line would help Knott End to develop into a holiday resort like Blackpool, this did not happen. The line began to lose money and, in 1930, the LMS which owned it, closed it to passenger traffic.

Garstang – For 600 years Garstang (which has a Norse name) has been a market centre for moss farmers and a meeting place for both the farmers and the hill folk to the east of the mosses. A Roman Road crosses the Wyre at Garstang: the 18th century turnpike road used the route the Romans had pioneered.

Garstang serves a district that is almost wholly agricultural and for this reason has maintained a fairly constant population over the past two centuries, unlike many other places in Lancashire which have seen their populations explode.

For many centuries two annual fairs were held in Garstang, and they played an important role in the local economy. But by the mid-19th century the June fair had been discontinued. The November fair, where, on three successive days sheep, cattle and horses were traded, continued until the First World War, when it, too, was discontinued.

Thursday is Garstang's market day and, like the fairs, it had its beginnings in antiquity. By the reign of Charles II, Garstang's market had gained a wide reputation for selling wool yarn, grain, cattle and fish. The market continues today with market stalls still being erected in the street.

REFRESHMENTS:
There are numerous possibilities in Garstang.

Walk 13   THE DRUMLIN   2m (3km)

Maps: OS Sheets Landranger 102; Pathfinder 658.

An interesting circumambulation of a drumlin.

Start: At 355432, Wyreside Ecology Centre, Stanah.

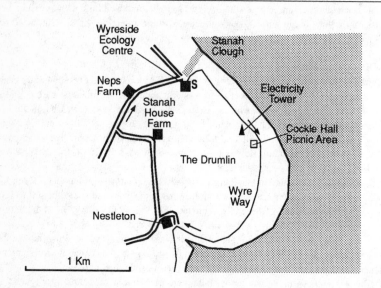

From the Centre, go diagonally left, across the car park, towards the estuary, joining the Wyre Way by turning left at a signpost and following a path, as directed by a Wyre Way signpost for Skippool. The path, which is sometimes subjected to flooding, is edged with a tapping rail for use by the blind and the partially sighted as far as **Cockle Hall picnic area**. Once past the picnic area the path curves to the right as it rounds **the Drumlin**: from it moorings are seen ahead and to the left. Continue to a signposted junction of routes. Turn right, following the sign 'To Underbank Road, 200 yards'. Go through a small gate to the side of a larger one, into a lane. Continue along the lane, which soon turns to the left and reaches a facing road.

Turn right, along Underbank Road, which has a tarmac surface and offers pleasant walking. Soon after passing Oakland Cottage, on the right, and just short of Stanah House Farm, the road turns sharp left. Stay with it, soon curving right to reach a

T-junction. Turn right along another minor road, soon reaching Stanah. Follow the road as it curves right, passing the Farm House Kitchen on the left, to reach the main entrance to the Wyre Estuary Country Park. Just inside, on the right, lies the Ecology Centre from where this varied walk began.

POINTS OF INTEREST:

Cockle Hall Picnic Area – This neat little picnic area looks across the river to Wardleys and the remains of an old ferry jetty. Travellers would summon the ferry by standing on the jetty and whistling or wildly waving their arms.

Cockle Hall was a tiny cottage, the only dwelling hereabouts. Its original tenant described himself as 'Th' only squire this side of the Wyre'. Although only small, Cockle Hall housed a family of 13 in the late 19th century.

The Drumlin – Drumlins are formed from the morainic deposits of glaciers. When a glacier continues to move as it melts, the boulder clay it deposits is not spread as a flat layer. It is smoothed and sculpted into rounded hills composed entirely of clay and boulders. These are the drumlins. This particular drumlin lies parallel to the River Wyre, on a north to south axis, its northern and steeper side pointing to face the flow of the glacier responsible for it. The northern end of the drumlin, where the Park's car park is sited, was originally steep, but has been levelled. The original steepness suggests that the glacier responsible for it came from across Morecambe Bay.

As the route of the walk edges the Wyre, it passes through an area where, in the past, exposures of boulder clay would be seen, the fresh clay and the pebbles having been brought to the surface by rabbits.

As the walk continues southwards, so the slopes of the drumlin become much gentler and lower. Here the exposed boulder clay, now becoming overgrown, has a reddish brown tint to it, due to staining by iron oxide. At the southern end of the drumlin the boulder clay contains pebbles, rather than boulders. Because they have been brought to the area, probably from the Lake District, in the glacier, and are not of local origin, these are called glacial erratics.

Because boulder clay is soft and does not provide a sound foundation for anything constructed on it the electricity tower near Cockle Hall picnic area stands on a foundation reinforced with sheet piling to prevent it slipping into the river.

REFRESHMENTS:
Farm House Kitchen, Stanah.

Walk 14   SLAIDBURN AND HIGHER HIGH FIELD   2½m (4km)

Maps: OS Sheets Landranger 103; Pathfinder 660.

A pleasant field walk with a double crossing of the River Hodder.

Start: At 714523, the car park on the eastern side of Slaidburn.

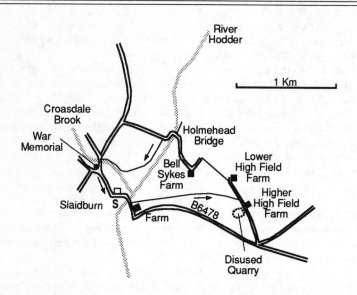

From the car park go left, along the road, to cross the **River Hodder**. Once over the bridge go through the second of two gates on the left, ignoring the stile beside the first one. Go straight ahead, uphill, passing a farm on the right. Go up a steep field, bearing left to follow a diagonal depression on the hillside. Leave the field over a stile about 10 yards to the right of the field corner. Cross the next field close to the fence on the left, turning left to cross a stile over it, and turning right to continue with the fence now on your right. On reaching a section of wall in the middle of a facing fence cross a step stile in it, to the right of a hawthorn bush. Cross the next field close to the wall on the right, leave it through a facing gate in its right-hand corner. Cross the next field to reach a ladder stile. Cross the field beyond, bearing slightly to the right to reach a stile. Go over and bear half-right across a field on a track which reaches a waymarked post. The arrows confirm your route. Turn left along a farm road, and where it bears right, into a farmyard, go slightly left to cross a waymarked stile. Walk through what appears to be a private garden but is, in fact, cultivated grassland, neatly lawned and spangled with trees and shrubs.

Go through a gate and walk straight ahead, pulling away slightly from a stream on your left, to follow a green track which passes to the right of a facing wall and continues close to the wall on the left. In the bottom left-hand corner of the field, turn left through a waymarked gate and continue along a lane. At the lane end go through a gate and turn right to pass in front of Bell Sykes farmhouse. Now turn left to a gate, to leave the farm. Go diagonally right, along a farm track, as directed by a yellow arrow, following it over a couple of fields to Holmehead Bridge, which spans the River Hodder. Leave the farm track through a facing gate and turn left, over the bridge. Now turn left along a lane, as directed by the yellow arrow. In a short distance leave the lane, turning left beside a wall on your right. At the end of the field go over a ladder stile and continue straight ahead along a track. In a short distance, bear right, away from the track and, where the wall on the right ends, go along a ridge which curves to the right to meet Croasdale Brook. Go along the riverbank to reach a kissing gate where a bridge spans the brook. Go through and turn left along a road. Turn left again at Slaidburn's war memorial and go through the village back to the car park.

POINTS OF INTEREST:

River Hodder – The Forest of Bowland is an area of steep hills and extensive moorland and from one of its lonely heights tiny sykes become becks and spill down cloughs, joining to become the lovely River Hodder. A little upstream of Stocks Reservoir the waters of Hazel Beck, flowing from Catlow Fell, meet it, as, lower down, does Bottoms Beck, which drains into the reservoir from Gisburn Forest. Croasdale Beck escapes from its cradle on the Croasdale Fells and meanders through a pleasing landscape, approaching Slaidburn along a delightful wooded valley and pours into the Hodder on the edge of this lovely village. Now firmly established, the Hodder flows merrily on to the Irish Sea.

REFRESHMENTS:
The Hark to Bounty Inn, Slaidburn.
The Eatery, at Slaidburn car park.

Walk 15   **Russells Farm**   2¹/₂m (4km)

Maps: OS Sheets Landranger 97; Pathfinder 650.

Pleasant field walking throughout: a slice of rural Lancashire.

Start: At 622687, Russells Farm, 1¹/₂ miles north-east of Wray.

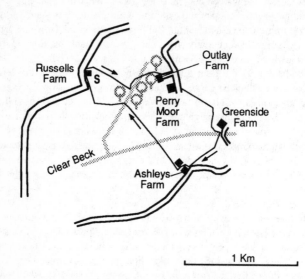

From the concrete entrance to the farmyard, turn left, through a gate, into a field and walk close to the hedge on the left, briefly, to reach a field corner. Turn right, still staying close to the hedge on the left, and descending to its far end. Turn left and cross a gap stile in a small section of wall. Go diagonally right across the field beyond, keeping above a wooded gill. Go over a stile near the right-hand end of a facing wall and walk ahead, keeping above the gill. As the land falls away ahead into a more open area, turn right and cross a brook on a culvert. Cross a fence and turn left at once to go along a climbing path, which, as it clears woodland, becomes broader and greener. Soon Outlay Farm is seen ahead. Pass close to the gable end of the farmhouse, ignoring the stile just past it and continuing, briefly, to the end of the wall on the right. There, turn right, leaving the field through a gate. Turn left along the farm road and, at its end, go right along a lane that climbs to Perry Moor Farm.

Go into the farmyard and turn left, leaving it through a gate. Cross the field beyond to reach a stile. Go over and head diagonally right, on rising ground, towards an, as yet unseen, right-hand corner of this large rough pasture. As this large field is crossed, a wicket is seen in the fence on the right, about 50 yards short of the field corner. Go through and walk close to the hedge on the left to reach a gateway at the corner of the hedge on the left. Do not go through it: instead, turn left, as the hedge does, and continue alongside it. At the field corner, from where Greenside Farm is seen on the left, ignore the facing gate and turn right, along the edge of the field, still staying near the hedge on the left as you climb towards the field corner. As a farm, Ashleys, comes into view to the right, go towards it, aiming for the field corner. There, go over a signed stile on to a road. Turn right for about 100 yards, then turn right again along a signed bridleway, passing to the right of the farm. The track leads to the back of the farm: turn left, between buildings which have been converted into dwellings and, on approaching a facing cottage, turn left briefly, then right. Soon after, go through a gate and, after a few feet, go through another gate into a field. Cross this close to the hedge on your left, exiting through a gate close to the field's left-hand corner.

Cross the field beyond, bearing slightly right as the fence curves left, downhill, to cross a brook at its foot. Keep ahead, walking parallel to the fence on your left, on rising ground. When the fence ends, keep ahead through a broken line of hawthorns. As this large field levels slightly, a building is seen ahead. Keep to the right of it and continue through a gate in a section of wall. Cross the next field aiming for the left-hand corner of the woodland ahead. Soon a gill containing a brook comes into view: at this point bear left towards a line of hawthorns and descend a track which crosses the brook on a culvert. Go through a facing gate and continue along the track, which curves left and goes diagonally up a steep bank. From the bank top continue close to the hedge on the left to reach a step stile in it. Do not cross this: instead, turn right, along a line of trees which once edged one side of a lane. Today it looks more like a ditch. On reaching Russells Farm, turn left through a gate and immediately right to exit the field through a gate on to a road. Turn right, in front of the farmhouse, to return to the start.

REFRESHMENTS:
Sorry! None on this walk, you will have to bring your own.

Walk 16   CROSSGILL AND LITTLEDALE HALL $2^1/_2$m (4km)

Maps: OS Sheets Landranger 97; Pathfinder 637.

A splendid mix of woodland paths and open country.

Start: At 559624, the eastern end of Crossgill hamlet.

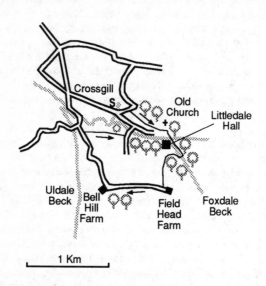

From the bridge over the stream to the east of Crossgill go eastwards, out of the hamlet, passing the entrance to Littledale Hall on the right. Continue uphill, and where the road goes around a hairpin bend to the left, go straight ahead over a stile. Go along a path through woodland to reach a stile waymarked with a yellow arrow. Go over and cross the field beyond, staying close to the wall/fence on the right to reach a waymarked gate. Go through and continue past an old church, now used as a farm store, on the left. Go through a waymarked gate and follow the wall on your right, bearing right and descending. Go through a gate, cross a bridge over a beck to reach Littledale Hall, to the right. Turn left, uphill, along a surfaced road, as directed by an arrow. At the hilltop turn right, between buildings, and, on reaching a facing one, turn left, briefly, to walk just past the building on the right. Now turn right through a

36

waymarked wicket and go along a path into woodland with Foxdale Beck below on the right.

Soon the path crosses the beck on a footbridge. A little further on, set well above deep bracken, a red arrow beckons: go straight ahead. The path levels out, then makes a sharp turn doubling back on itself, but now on the other side of the stream. Soon, turn sharp left and climb steeply, as directed by a white arrow. The path levels out, then leaves the wood over a stile. Go slightly right, climbing up a rough pasture along a faint path through rushes. Eventually the path fades away like the Cheshire cat, so simply continue in the same direction, still climbing.

On reaching the top of the hill, Field Head Farm is seen ahead. Go diagonally right and cross a step stile in the wall on the right, just short of a gate. Go diagonally left across the next field, aiming for the right-hand side of the farm buildings. Continue by edging along the side of the farm to reach a gate near a footpath sign. Turn right, along the farm road. From here the views are tremendous and embrace the vast spread of Morecambe Bay to the right and, to the left, Black Fell, a sea of purple heather in late August. Cross a cattle grid, continuing along the farm road which soon leads downhill to Bell Hill Farm. There it crosses another cattle grid and bears to the right, leaving the farm behind. Stay with the road, descending into the valley bottom in a series of turns to reach Uldale Beck. Within about 150 yards of where the farm road meets a minor road at a bend in the latter, close to where it bridges Uldale Beck, turn right, along a faint climbing track to reach a stile beside a gate. Follow the track through woodland. Just after crossing the head of a pronounced gill on the left the track begins to curve left. On reaching a lane at right angles, turn left, descending through trees to reach a bridge over Foxdale Beck. Turn left along a surfaced road to leave the grounds of Littledale Hall, from the entrance of which the end of the walk is seen a few yards ahead.

REFRESHMENTS:
Sorry, none on this route, so you must bring your own.

Walk 17   BLAKE HALL   2¹/₂m (4km)

Maps: OS Sheets Landranger 102; Pathfinder 679.
A fascinating field walk through pleasing countryside.
Start: At 539382, the entrance to Blake Hall.

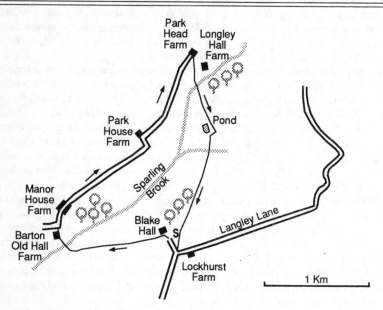

Go along the lane towards the Hall, soon passing a bungalow on the left. Just beyond
it Blake Hall Farm is reached. From the concrete forecourt to the farm, cross a
waymarked stile on the left and follow the fence on the right across the field beyond.
Cross a fence close to the right-hand corner, beside a sycamore tree where the word
'footpath' can be seen written on the fence. Now stay close to the fence on your left to
reach a stile over it. Go over and turn right to continue in the same direction, now with
the fence on your right. A stile is soon reached on the right. Go over and turn left,
soon crossing a footbridge over Sparling Brook. Now bear right up a sloping field
towards Barton Old Hall Farm ahead.

On reaching a facing fence, turn right along it, passing a large slurry tank. Now
turn left along a track into the farmyard, exiting through a gate. Turn right, through

Manor House farmyard, and continue along a lane to Park House Farm. Immediately in front of the farmhouse turn right, over a stile in the hedge on the right, and turn left along a farm track close to fence/hedge on the left. Go through a gate close to the left-hand corner of the field and continue along the track, which edges a second field and then crosses a third one to reach Park Head Farm. The track enters the farm through a gate and continues, muddily, past farm buildings and a large silage pit on the right. Where the track splits, go right, between farm buildings and, on the left, houses. Once past these, turn right through a gate, into a rough field. Turn right along the fence to the right, leaving the field over a stile. Immediately cross a brook on a rather old footbridge and keep ahead along a grassy path close to a fence and trees on the right. On reaching a step in the fence, continue up the bank ahead and cross a field, aiming for the near side of a line of tall trees.

Go through a gate towards the left-hand corner of a hawthorn hedge. The farm on the left is called Longley Hall. Go diagonally left across the field ahead, keeping to the left of a pond. Go through a gate in a hawthorn hedge and, just beyond, you will reach a crossing cart track. Turn right along it, soon turning left, with it, to cross a field to reach a bridge over Sparling Brook.

Cross the field beyond, leaving the now green track when it curves left, keeping ahead, then bearing slightly right to cross a stile. Go straight ahead across the next field, keeping to the left of a wooded area that protrudes into the field and then walking along the crest of the field. Go over a stile in the right-hand corner and cross the large field beyond, bearing to the left, using, as a guide, a line of trees, on the horizon, that has a dip in the middle. Aim for the dip, continuing to climb. Once the top of the ridge has been crossed, start to descend, maintaining direction to go through a gateway. Cross a little brook and climb, quite steeply, up the next field, maintaining direction. On reaching the brow of the hill, Lockhurst Farm can be seen a little to the left. Keep to the right of the farm, aiming towards the field's right-hand corner. There, go over a signed stile on to the road where the walk began.

REFRESHMENTS:
Sorry! There are none on this route.

Walk 18   **BARKER BROW AND WHITE HOLME**   2¹/₂m (4km)

Maps: OS Sheets Landranger 103; Pathfinder 680.

A gentle field walk in the lovely Ribble valley.

Start: At 663350, the car park on Barker Brow.

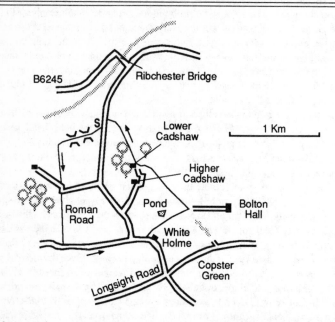

From the car park, cross a stile and go westwards across a field, crossing two footbridges to reach a facing track. Turn left, along the track, but after a short distance, where it turns sharp left, turn right, into a field, and immediately turn left to walk along a hedge. Maintain direction, crossing two stiled fields as you follow the course of a **Roman Road**, to meet a rough track end on. Follow this track for a short distance to where it makes a sharp turn to the left. Here leave it, keeping straight ahead to go over a stile to the right of a gatepost into a field with a telegraph pole in it. Walk past the telegraph post, leaving the field over another stile.

     Now aim for the right-hand corner of the next field and, keeping in the same direction and still on the course of the Roman Road, pass Showley Hall Farm over on the right. Go through a gap in the hedge on your right, and at once turn left. In a short distance you join a track: turn left along it, following it to a road, the B6245. Turn right, soon approaching White Holme Farm on the left. Just before the farm, turn left, over a stile. Walk past the farm, to your right, then go diagonally right across two fields, passing to the right of a small pond. About 200 yards past the pond, turn left over a stile to join, end on, a lane coming towards you from Bolton Hall. Turn left, following a stiled path and soon passing Higher Cadshaw Farm on the left. A little further on, cross a rough track, met at right angles, and descend into a shallow valley. On reaching a facing hedge turn left, along it, passing Lower Cadshaw Farm on your left. Go through a waymarked gate, and, at once, turn right along a path which will take you to the B6245. Turn left to return to the car park on **Barker Brow**.

POINTS OF INTEREST:

Barker Brow – Cowslips, in profusion, grow at Barker Brow and Himalayan balsam is well established along the edge of the nearby River Ribble. A very attractive gabled house, built in 1665, by a member of the Talbot family, stands close to Barker Brow. The family badge of a hunting hound is displayed above the front door.

Roman Road – Part of this pleasant walk follows the course of an old Roman Road that leads to Ribchester from the south. Ribchester is sited just across the Ribble from Barker Brow and was built, in about 75AD, as one of a chain of military stations. As the Romans developed the northern part of the country, so Ribchester increased in its importance. This road to it was part of a system of communications between Hadrian's Wall and Chester, where the legion had its headquarters.

During the second century, a force of Sarmatians, heavy cavalry troops from the lower Danube, was sent to Britain by Marcus Aurelius and many were stationed at *Bremetennacum*, as Ribchester was called by the Romans. These horsemen, classed as auxiliary troops, were considered to be more suitable than foot soldiers for controlling this sort of district. When they had completed their tour of duty, many chose to settle in the Ribble valley.

REFRESHMENTS:
The De Tabley Arms, the B6245 near Ribchester bridge.
Park Gate Inn, Copster Green.

Walk 19 COPSTER GREEN AND HARWOOD FOLD 2¹/₂m (4km)

Maps: OS sheets Landranger 103; Pathfinder 680.
Pleasant walking through the lovely Ribble Valley.
Start: At 675337, Copster Green village green.

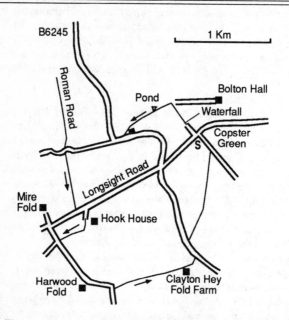

From the village green in the middle of Copster Green cross Longsight Road, which runs through the village, and follow a path that descends to a waterfall. Go over a stile on the left and along a path that climbs out of the shallow valley and then runs straight ahead. When, after almost a ¹/₄ mile, the end of a lane that leads off right to Bolton Hall is reached, turn left, over a stile, into a field. Walk along the field edge to the right, passing to the left of a pond in about 200 yards. Beyond, leave the field, going straight across the next field and curving left to skirt White Holme Farm. Go over a stile on to the B6245.

Turn right, but where it does a sharp right turn, go straight ahead, along a track. Continue for about 400 yards, then just after the track makes a sharp turn left and then another turn to the right, go over a stile on the left and walk straight ahead, along the route of an old **Roman Road**, soon reaching Longsight Road. As a guide, before the road is reached Mire Fold Farm can be seen on the right. Turn left along the road, with care, but soon turn right along the road to Nook House Farm. There, turn right, through a gap in a hedge, and go straight across the fields ahead to reach a track. Turn left, at a kennels sign, along the track, following it past Harwood Fold. A little beyond the farm, where the track makes a right-angled turn to the right, keep straight ahead, cross a stone stile. Now bear slightly left, keeping close to the hedge on your left. The farm on your right as you approach the B6245 ahead is Clayton Hey Fold. On reaching the main road, turn left, along it, for a short distance to reach a waymarked footpath on the right. Turn along this and, at its far end, turn left along a lane to return to the village green. Ahead on the final section of the walk there is a superb view of **Pendle Hill**.

POINTS OF INTEREST:

Roman Road – Ribchester, or Breme*tennacum* as the Romans knew it, is set among farms in a pleasant landscape of smiling meadowland and golden cornfields laced with leafy hedgerows. This pastoral scenery, part of Lancashire's fair face, is entirely free from the murk of industrialisation, and its flora and fauna are a joy to behold. Salmon swim in the River Ribble hereabouts and herons in profusion fish the shallows. In late springtime and early summer, the whole area is alive with glorious birdsong, May being the month of greatest birdsong.

Perhaps the most important find unearthed at Ribchester was a most attractive embossed bronze parade helmet and mask. It was discovered in 1795 and is now in the British Museum. The one on display at Ribchester is a copy.

Pendle Hill – Rising to 1827 feet (577 metres) the hill is one of Lancashire's most famous landmarks. Towering above the Ribble valley, it offers superb views of Bowland's wild fells and embraces the full length of Ribblesdale from the Yorkshire heights to the coast.

REFRESHMENTS:
The Park Gate Inn, Copster Green.

Walk 20 **ABBEY VILLAGE AND MILLSTONE EDGE** 2½m (4km)
Maps: OS Sheets Landranger 103; Pathfinder 689.
A fine airy walk using ancient ways.
Start: At 644224, the Hare and Hounds Inn, Abbey Village.

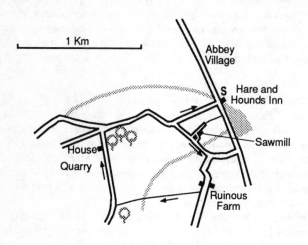

From the Inn, at the south-east end of Abbey Village, turn left along the footpath edging the A675. Some 50 yards after passing a 40 mph sign, turn right, crossing the road, with care, and going over a waymarked stile into a field. Walk beside the field's right edge, following a line of hawthorn trees and the remains of an old wall to reach the field's right-hand corner. Now go straight ahead, along a walled lane. At the lane end, go through a kissing gate into a sawmill's yard. Go forward for a few yards, then turn left to a concrete area. Turn right out of the sawmill yard into a lane and turn left, along it, to reach a junction on the right. Turn right here, through a gate, and follow a rough, but easy to follow, track, crossing rough pasture. On reaching a facing gate, go over a waymarked stile to the left and continue along the still climbing track. Soon the track goes through the remains of an old farm, the only building standing being the outside privy.

Continue along the track which has now sunk and has the remains of a wall on the left. At a point where the track starts to have a wall on both sides, turn right and continue beside a ruinous wall on the left. Where the wall bears left and becomes the left-hand wall of an overgrown walled lane, continue straight ahead, going through the remains of a gateway in the right-hand wall of the lane. Go diagonally left across a rough pasture, aiming for a little gill at the pasture's top right-hand corner. On reaching the corner of the field, continue along the remains of a lane, then cross a step stile in a facing fence. Go forward for a few yards to reach a stream: the easiest way to cross is to turn left, along the stream for a short distance to reach a well-used crossing point. Once over the stream, climb a steep bank, cross the remains of a wall and go straight ahead, climbing to level ground as a heather-clad moor is crossed. Continue along a narrow, but clear, path through the heather, aiming to the right of a solitary tree. When almost level with this tree the path reaches a facing, ruinous wall: cross this and walk beside another ruinous wall on your right.

Soon a very clear track is reached at right angles: turn right, along it, descending for almost $^1/_2$ mile to leave the moor over a waymarked stile to the left of a facing gate. Continue along a descending rough track, soon passing a detached house on the left. Continue along a tarmac lane, and at its end, turn right, along a road, soon reaching the road from **Abbey Village** to Withnell at a tangent. Cross the road to join a roadside footpath and go right, eastwards along it, for about $^1/_2$ mile to reach the A675. Cross, with care, to regain the starting Inn.

POINTS OF INTEREST:
Abbey Village – In common with much of Lancashire towards the end of the 18th century, Abbey Village had a mixed economy, with families drawing their livelihood from both industry and agriculture. Hand-loom weaving became a very important part of village life and Abbey Village also had a huge cotton mill. Yet, at that time there were still many families who relied entirely on agriculture for a living.

REFRESHMENTS:
The Hare and Hounds, Abbey Village.

Walk 21   PARK BRIDGE AND COPY NOOK FARM   3m (5km)

Maps: OS Sheets Landranger 103; Pathfinder 670.

A pleasant walk along quiet lanes and over heather moors with good views throughout.

Start: At 883463, on the Barnoldswick side of Park Bridge.

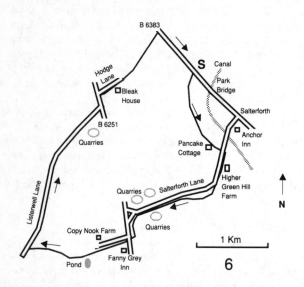

Go over the sturdier of two stiles, the one nearer the town, and cross a pasture, following the curve of a cutting containing the Leeds to Liverpool Canal and aiming for a stile that soon comes into view in a fence corner, slightly to the right. Cross the stile, ascend a meadow diagonally towards a section of drystone wall, seen from the brow of the hill, and cross a stile into a pasture. Cross directly to a stile, and cross another field, going along a low wall on your left. The path continues between Pancake Cottage, and a boundary wall to the left of it, to join a lane. Go along this lane to join Salterforth Lane over a cattle grid. Continue past Higher Greenhill Farm on the left. The tarmac lane curves to the right, between disused quarries, and climbs steeply: where it splits to form a green triangle, take the left fork, briefly, to join the B6251 and continue along it to a footpath sign on the opposite side of the road close to the Fanny Grey Inn.

46

Follow the sign along a heavily wooded lane towards Gisburn Old Road. At the bottom of the lane, Copy Nook Farm is passed on the right. Continue through a metal gate, cross a pasture and go over a facing stone stile into a large field. Cross this, bearing right uphill to a gateway and passing, across the moor on your left, a small pond. Go through a gate on to a heather moor to follow a track, and cross a stile near a gate in a facing wall. Beyond, descend to Listerwell's walled lane. Turn right downhill, eventually reaching the B6251 at the top of Tubber Hill. Cross the road and turn left, towards Barnoldswick, seen below. Soon, turn right along Hodge Lane, descending, then levelling, and passing Bleak House on the right. Where the lane ends at a gate, go over an adjacent stile and down a green lane until the wall on your left goes left. Here ignore the path going right to left and continue straight ahead, passing a mound on which a Scots Pine grows. Soon the path descends King Hill to a stile. Cross on to the B6383 and turn right towards **Salterforth** along a roadside footpath back to the start.

POINTS OF INTEREST:

Salterforth – With its immaculately kept cottages, Salterforth has won the 'Best Kept Village In Lancashire' award on more than one occasion.

From a raised bank on the left of the lane to Gisburn Old Road there are excellent views towards Craven and the Yorkshire Dales.

REFRESHMENTS:

The Fanny Grey, Salterforth.
The Anchor Inn, Salterforth.

Walk 22   RYAL FOLD AND JUBILEE TOWER   3m (5km)

Maps: OS Sheets Landranger 103; Pathfinder 689.

Breezy moorland walking with lots of good views.

Start: At 666215, the car park opposite Tockholes Nature Trail.

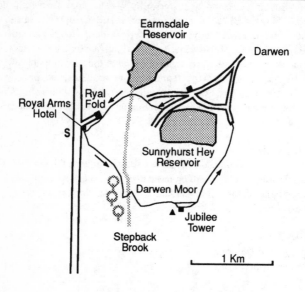

From the car park, near the Royal Arms Hotel, turn left, as waymarked, past the end of Hollinstead Terrace. After a few yards, before reaching the cottages, turn right, through a kissing gate into a field and climb along a track. On reaching a gate, cross a stile to the left and continue through woodland. Where the track descends, ignore the stile ahead, turning sharp left with the track, but after a few yards, cross a stile beside a gate on the right and go left, as directed by a carving of the Jubilee Tower on a stone. At another Jubilee Tower indicator, turn right to climb steeply along a narrow track to reach a seat. Here, there is a track fork: take the left-hand branch, as directed by another Jubilee Tower indicator. The path cuts through rough pasture to reach a stile – a most considerate one, with a useful flap to allow dogs to go underneath – on to the moor. Go over and turn left, edging the moor close to the fence on the left. Where the path splits, keep straight ahead on the higher, right-hand branch, as directed by another Jubilee Tower indicator.

The **Jubilee Tower** now comes into view ahead. As the path passes to the left of it, take a right-hand path that leads directly to it, passing a nearby trig. point. From the tower take a path which descends north-eastwards to join the one you left on approaching the tower. You join where the path splits: take the left-hand branch, descending to go along a wall on the right. On reaching a small gate beside a larger one, bear left, descending along an unsurfaced road. After about 100 yards turn left along a walled lane, leaving it over a gap stile. Continue across the field beyond, going along a green track to reach a facing fence. Turn left, as signed, for a few yards, then turn right. Continue straight ahead, briefly, then bear right to return to the original footpath, having made a short, official, detour. On reaching a concrete waterworks road, turn right to descend along it. At the road end turn left along a tarmac road. Soon, in front of a house on the right, the road forks: take the higher, left-hand branch. The road climbs quite steeply, then levels out: just past the entrance to an enclosure on the left, turn right down a green fenced lane. Go through a revolving stile in the right-hand corner of the facing wall and bear slightly right to descend a pasture. Go through a gateway in the facing fence and bear right across a narrow field ahead, leaving over a stile. Follow a path across the next field, crossing a stream, to reach a kissing gate. Beyond this the path curves slightly to go along the field's edge, staying close to a fence on the left. At the top end of the field, go over a stile near a gate and continue to a wicket in a facing corner. Turn left, but instead of going up the lane ahead, bear left and go through a gateway, passing to the front of a house on the right. Go through a wicket to the left of a gate into a field and cross diagonally left towards the left end of a terrace. Go through a kissing gate, turn right and go along the front of the terrace. Turn right at the end to return to the car park.

POINTS OF INTEREST:

Jubilee Tower – The tower was erected in 1898 to commemorate the Diamond Jubilee of Queen Victoria. An anti-clockwise spiral staircase leads to a balcony from where another climbs to the top. From the top, the views are very impressive.

REFRESHMENTS:
The Royal Arms Hotel, Ryal Fold.

Walk 23   GRINDLETON AND FOXLEY BANK   3m (5km)

Maps: OS Sheets Landranger 103; Pathfinder 669.

A delightful mix of quiet road, field and riverside.

Start: At 759455, the Buck Inn, Grindleton.

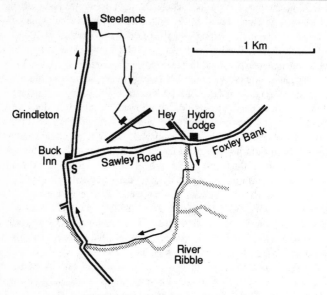

Go northwards through Grindleton, following the road for almost $\frac{1}{2}$ mile to reach Steelands Farm. Turn right through the farmyard, as waymarked, exiting through a gate and immediately turning right through another gate. Descend the field beyond and turn left along the far hedge to reach a stile in the corner. Go over and turn right to reach a little step in the hedge on the right. Cross and follow the mix of fence and hawthorn on your right. Where this turns sharp right, continue ahead to rejoin a fence at a corner. Bear right along a fence to reach a stile. Go over and bear left to walk beside the fence (now on your left) along a sunken track. Go over a stile in the left-hand corner of a facing hedge and turn right, staying close to the hedge on the right. Soon, at another step in the field, cross a step stile and walk ahead along a sunken track, close to a hawthorn hedge on the left. At the track's end cross a stile and immediately turn left. In a few yards cross a stile on the left, to the right of a gate.

Descend the field beyond, bearing slightly left to cross a stile to the left of a farm building. Cross a narrow lane, go over another stile and walk straight ahead over a little paddock, leaving over a stile in the facing hawthorn hedge, to the left of a gate. Go over a farm lane and cross another stile into a field. Cross, diagonally left along a cart track leading to a gateway in the hedge on the left. Do not go through the gateway: instead, turn right and continue along the hedge on the left. As it curves to the left, a gate with a stile alongside it comes into view. Cross the stile and continue in the same direction across the next field, staying close to a hawthorn hedge on the left.

On reaching a gate in the field corner do not go through: instead, turn right and walk along the hawthorn hedge on the left. When the hedge turns left, do likewise, and on approaching the field corner, bear slightly to the right to reach a stile in the hedge coming in from the right. Go diagonally left, downhill, across the field beyond to reach a signed stile to the left of a sycamore tree. Go over and turn left along a mix of hedge and fence on the left, passing a most beautiful house, Hey, on the left. Just past it, in the field corner, go over a stile into a lane and turn right along it to join the Sawley road. Turn left, passing Hydro Lodge on the left. As the road bends left, turn right, as waymarked, to join the Ribble Way. Cross a field to a gap between trees. Go over a step stile to the left of a ghyll, with the River Ribble now just in front of you. Walk towards it, bearing right and keeping above the ghyll. At the bottom of the field, cross a stile close to its right-hand corner.

Cross a bridge over the feeder you have just followed and immediately turn left, guided by a Ribble Way sign, alongside the feeder to reach the Ribble. Turn right along the **riverbank**. On reaching a facing fence, go right, along it, to reach a stile. Go over and continue downstream, crossing several stiles and, at times, walking on top of a dyke, built to prevent flooding. On reaching a bridge over the Ribble, leave the riverside through a gate and continue along the road, keeping straight ahead at a road junction to return to the Inn.

POINTS OF INTEREST:
Riverbank – Oystercatchers, mallard, gulls, swallows, pied wagtails and herons abound along the riverside.

REFRESHMENTS:
The Buck Inn, Grindleton.

Walk 24   SLAIDBURN AND SHAY HOUSE   3m (5km)

Maps: OS Sheets Landranger 103; Pathfinder 660.

A close look at Croasdale Brook.

Start: At 712524, the Slaidburn War Memorial.

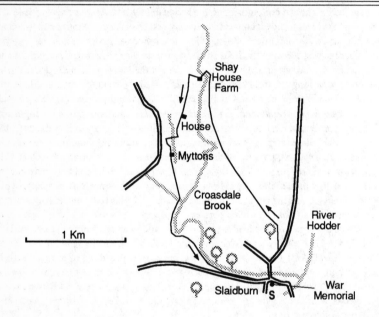

From the War Memorial take the road northwards, soon crossing Croasdale Brook. Continue along the road which begins to climb and curve to the right. Turn left over a stile on to path signed 'To Croasdale' and go diagonally right, uphill, as waymarked. As you climb this steep, outcrop strewn bank, aim for the left-hand sign of a facing wall, where there is a waymarker. Continue climbing alongside a hedge of trees on your right, as directed, towards a copse. Go through this copse of tall beeches, exiting over a stile. Follow the edge of the field beyond to reach another yellow arrow waymarker. Now go diagonally left, crossing a field on rising ground, aiming, at first, at a white house slightly left and on the horizon. When a stile comes into view aim for it. Go over and cross the field beyond. Keep on the ridge top, leaving the field over a waymarked stile. Go straight across the next field to reach a stile in a wall. From here

Stocks Reservoir can be seen in the distance. Now descend slightly left across a field, keeping close to a line of hawthorns on your right, to reach a waymarked stile. Go over and cross the next field staying, at first, close to the wall on the left. When the wall curves left, walk ahead to reach a stile in a facing wall. Cross the next field to reach a stile in a corner.

Turn left, over a bridge, and walk to Shay House Farm. Go to the right of the buildings, through a signed, broad gate and cross a field, staying close to the wall on the right to reach a gate. Go through and follow the broad lane beyond to go reach a gate in the left-hand corner of the facing wall. Follow the track beyond which curves right, uphill. When you are opposite a gate in the wall on the right, leave the track by turning left, and go straight up a field to a stile. Go over and follow a mix of fence and hedge on the left, to where there is a step in it. Here, keep straight ahead, on a path towards a house. Go through a gate to the right of the house and descend diagonally right across a field to reach a stream close to 'Bridge End'. Go through a wicket to the right of the house and turn right to bridge the stream. Go through a gate and turn left, over a stile, into a field. Cross diagonally right towards Myttons Farm. Leave the field to the left of the single storey building, cross a forecourt and go through the middle one of three gates into a walled lane, as directed by a yellow arrow. Turn left at the lane end to go alongside a wall on the left. Go through a gate at the end of the field and go diagonally right, across the field beyond on a green path which leads to a stream. Cross the stream on a clapper bridge and, in a few yards, go over a stile. Continue down the field beyond, with Croasdale Beck on your left.

Go over a stile at the field's end and continue close to a fence on your left, pulling away from the brook. Half-way along the fence a footpath sign confirms your route as you rejoin the stream which has curved away and back. Follow the brook-side path to a stile. Go over and continue along the path back to Slaidburn.

REFRESHMENTS:
The Hark to Bounty Inn, Slaidburn.

Maps: OS Sheets Landranger 97; Pathfinder 650.
Riverside walking where the Hindburn and Roeburn meet.
Start: At 602677, the Methodist Chapel, Wray.

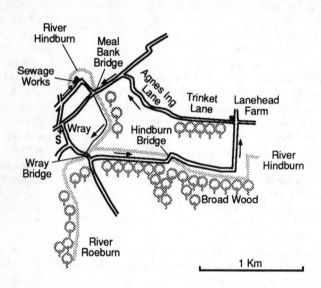

From the chapel in **Wray** go diagonally left, across the road (the B6480), and continue along Kiln Lane to where it splits into three. Here turn right, along another lane which soon leads to a sewage works. At this point one lane goes to the left of the works, another goes to its right, while a third, narrower and more overgrown, lane goes right.

Take the latter lane and at its end go straight up a bank to reach a road where it crosses the River Hindburn on Meal Bank bridge. Cross the road and continue along a riverside path. After a short distance a weir is passed, above which the river makes a huge sweep, curving to the right. The way is along the riverside and round the inside of this huge curve. Once it has been rounded cross a stile and continue along the riverbank. Just beyond the stile and short of reaching another one at the end of the next field is the confluence of two rivers, **the Hindburn and the Roeburn**.

Soon, Wray Bridge, which spans the Roeburn, comes into view. On reaching it, turn left and cross the bridge. After $\frac{1}{2}$ mile, cross the river on Hindburn bridge and continue for a further $\frac{1}{3}$ mile where the road turns sharp left. At the next cross-roads, turn left into Trinket Lane, passing Lanehead Farm, on the right, and alongside a wood, on the left. After another $\frac{1}{2}$ mile, the lane curves right and passes two farms to continue, now as Agnes Ing Lane, to a T-junction. Here, turn left back into Wray village to return to the chapel and the start.

POINTS OF INTEREST:

Wray – The village's name is derived from the Scandinavian 'vra' which means 'an out of the way corner'. The village is as pretty as a picture, all peace and harmony and neat as a new pin. Some of the cottages close to the river are set back behind long gardens, while others nearer the middle of the village push outwards to edge narrow footpaths. A lamp post, held by a cherubic figure, is a delight. It was erected to commemorate Queen Victoria's Jubilee in 1887, and was originally a gas lamp, though it is now electric. A tree-lined avenue leads down to the village church, which has two bells in an open steeple. Part of the Methodist Chapel was once a Quaker meeting house and a row of houses built in 1988 is called Meeting House Row, all of which just goes to show that religion, in many forms, played an important part in Wray life.

At one time a hundred people were employed in a silk mill in Wray, spinning raw silk which came from China via the docks at Lancaster. At that time silk hat making was an important local industry.

The Hindburn and Roeburn Rivers – The area around Wray is a walkers' paradise, in particular the country close to these two rivers, which are the haunts of dippers, sandpipers, grey and pied wagtails, swallows and many other birds. Primroses, wood anemones and Herb Robert bloom along the riverbank and in the woodlands through which the Hindburn and the Roeburn rivers flow from their respective cradles in the nearby fells where the Cantsfields, the Harringtons and other Lonsdale lords had their hunting preserves.

REFRESHMENTS:
The New Inn, Wray.
The George and Dragon, Wray.

Walk 26   FENISCOWLES PAPER MILLS   3m (5km)

Maps: OS Sheets Landranger 103; Pathfinder 689.

Easy walking: outwards along the canal towpath, returning alongside the River Darwen.

Start: At 624252, Finnington's Marina, Riley Green.

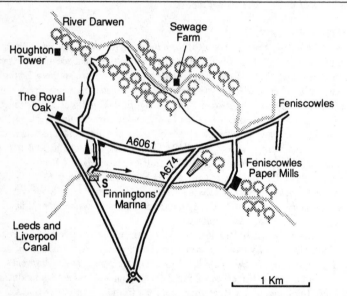

From the Marina turn right along the roadside pavement, cross the canal bridge and immediately turn right, through a gate and down a slope to the Leeds and Liverpool Canal towpath. Go eastwards along the towpath, soon going under bridge No. 918. Soon the canal curves to the right and the tall chimney of the paper mill is seen ahead. Go under a second, unnumbered, bridge, beyond which the canal makes another right curve. Before the next bridge is reached, you will see a concrete boundary fence on the left: leave the towpath just short of this fence and descend a path to join a broader path. Turn left along this, ignoring a gate on the right. Go downhill along the path which leads to the paper mill. Go forward to the checkout and turn left to leave the mill through the main entrance. Walk along the road to its T-junction with the A674. Turn left, using a roadside footpath to reach an old boundary stone for 'Black-Burn

Hundred, Leyland Hundred'. There, cross the road diagonally left, with great care, to reach a signed lane the left-hand end of a terrace. The lane climbs steadily: where it levels out, turn left over a stile and walk close to a fence on the right, at first, maintaining direction across a field where it ends to reach a stile. Go over and turn left along the fence to reach a stile. Go over and cross the next field, bearing right to a stile. Go over and bear left on a path through woodland. The path descends towards the River Darwen, then turns left to continue alongside and a little above it.

Leave the wood over a stile and follow the edge of a field along the riverbank as it describes a large arc. As a wooded bank is approached, turn from the river to join a track which curves right, up the bank, to reach a gate. Cross a stile to the right and continue up the track through a field to reach a gate. To the right here is **Hoghton Tower**. Go through a kissing gate beside on to a lane and turn left to reach the A6061. Cross, with care, and turn left along a roadside path. Just past the entrance to a BBC radio station, turn right along a signed lane past derelict Deerbolt Cottage. The lane leads to the canal towpath, reaching it opposite the Boatyard Inn. Turn right to retrace your steps back to the start.

POINTS OF INTEREST:

Hoghton Tower – Sited on a wooded hill above the River Darwen, the Tower was built in 1562 by Thomas Hoghton. In 1946 it became one of the first historic houses to be opened to the public.

REFRESHMENTS:
The Boatyard Inn, Riley Green.
The Royal Oak Inn, Riley Green.

Walk 27   CALDER VALE   3m (5km)

Maps: OS Sheets Landranger 102; Pathfinder 668.

A pleasant glimpse of Calder Vale.

Start: At 531453, the war memorial in Calder Vale village.

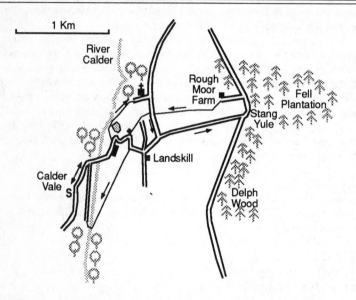

From the war memorial turn right, along the road, descending and staying on it as it curves right to bridge the River Calder. Beyond, the road curves left, climbing in front of a row of cottages on the right. Just past these, go through a gap beside a facing gate into woodland. Follow a tarmac footpath which soon edges a millpond on the right. The River Calder is below, on the left. Just beyond a weir, the path bears right, away from the river, climbing through woodland, and becoming steeper as it curves to continue just inside the wood's edge.

The path exits the wood, reaching the church of St John the Evangelist, beyond which a school is passed on the left. Continue along a road, briefly, and turn right at a T-junction, going along an unsurfaced farm road, passing a farm on the left and curving left, uphill, beyond it. Go through a gateway and cross the next field close to a wall on the right. The farm road continues through a gate and stays close to the wall on the

58

right through the next field. On leaving the field, the road, now surfaced, curves right. Before this curve, turn left through a gate into a field, and follow a rough field track alongside the wall on the left.

The track climbs steadily towards a plantation on the horizon: go through a facing metal gate, continuing along the track to exit through another gate in the left-hand corner of a facing wall. Continue across a field, still on the track, passing a pond and going through a facing gate on to a minor road. Turn left along the road which soon curves left, before continuing straight as an arrow. Before it curves left again, go left, over a cattle grid and along the lane to Rough Moor Farm.

On approaching the farm, turn left over a stile in a fence and go diagonally right down the field. Now walk beside a brook and close to a fence on the right. Near the bottom of the field, bear left to go through a gate in a facing fence. Do not go over the ladder stile on the right: instead, continue down the field, walking parallel to the wall on your right. At the far end, turn right, along the farm track used on the outward leg. Go through a gate into the farm area, turn left, and go over a stile. Cross the field beyond, staying close to the wall on the left. Exit over a stile in the left-hand corner of a facing fence and cross the next field, again staying close to the wall on the left. As the end of the field is reached, go diagonally right to reach a stile at the right-hand side of a section of facing wall, where it joins a line of trees. Go over and cross the field beyond, staying close to the hedge on the left, but pulling away from it as it curves left. Now aim for a gate in a fence at the back of some cottages. Go to the left of Stirk Hey Cottage and immediately turn left along a concrete road. At its end turn right, through a gate, and go along a short concrete lane into a field. Cross diagonally left, aiming for an electricity pole alongside a solitary tree just across a ditch. There, turn right and go over a stile in a facing hedge.

Cross the next field diagonally left, and on reaching the rim of the valley that cradles the River Calder, continue in the same direction, descending through rushes to reach the river to the left of a solitary oak that fronts some electricity wires. Soon the river comes into view: cross it on a footbridge and immediately climb steps on to a road. Turn right, along it, going through riverside woodland. At the end of the road, turn left along the minor road used on the outward leg, going uphill back to the war memorial.

REFRESHMENTS:
Sorry, none on this one.

Walk 28   **Skippool and Little Thornton**   3m (5km)
Maps: OS Sheets Landranger 102; Pathfinder 658.
A pleasant walk with an exciting blend of old and new.
Start: At 357409, Skippool car park.

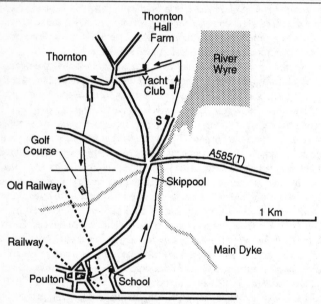

From the car park, turn left, following the route of the Wyre Way, passing the River
House Restaurant and the **Blackpool and Fleetwood Yacht Club**, then continuing
along a riverside path for almost $1/4$ mile. Now turn left, leaving the Wyre Way, to
follow a path signed for Little Thornton. At the top of a rise Thornton Hall Farm is
reached: go past it and follow Woodhouse Road to the B5412. Cross and turn left
along Tarn Road. This soon curves right and heads towards Thornton: before reaching
the town, turn left along Links Gate Lane. Go over a stile and walk ahead to reach the
A585(T). Cross, with great care, and continue southwards, following a path, signed
by a finger post. Pass to the left of a pond and keep to the left of a hedge to reach a
waymarked post at a facing path. Bear slightly left, beside a ditch and a hedge, to
reach a footbridge over a stream. Cross and turn right towards a tall hedge. Walk
beside it to a stile and go over on to the track bed of the old Preston and Wyre Railway.

Go left to reach Breck Road, going right, briefly, along it then left, at the Royal Oak Inn, into Station Road. After some 500 yards a railway bridge is reached: turn left, along a path to Howarth Crescent. Continue along this, and at its far end cross a footbridge over a partly filled cutting to reach Moorland Road. Turn right, then left at a T-junction into Little Poulton Lane. Go along the lane, passing **Little Poulton Hall**, and at its end go over a stile. Walk close to the hedge on your right to reach another stile. Go over and cross the field beyond, as directed by a waymarker, to reach Main Dyke. Continue northwards along this to reach a stile into a wooded area. Walk past the backs of houses and a caravan site, on the left, to reach the A585(T). Turn left, with care, passing the River Wyre Hotel to reach a roundabout. Turn right into Wyre Road, passing Thornton Lodge Hotel and an old house, Tarn Hows, on the way back to the car park.

POINTS OF INTEREST:

Blackpool and Fleetwood Yacht Club – In the 1870's the site now occupied by the Yacht Club was acquired by Silcock's, who built a bone mill there. Animal bones were shipped here for processing into bonemeal. In 1947 the factory was demolished when the business was transferred to larger premises in Liverpool. However, so legend has it, the ghost of one of the mill's Victorian workmen remains to remind yachtsmen of the original use of the club's premises.

Little Poulton Hall – Little Poulton is a very pleasant hamlet, a fine mixture of old and new. Little Poulton Hall, to the east of the hamlet, is not the original mansion: that stood on land nearby. The history of the present hall is a long one. In 1570 it was occupied by George Hesketh, who married Dorothy Westby of Mowbreck. Their son, William, married Elizabeth Allen of Rossall Hall. The Heskeths of Mains Hall continued to be associated with Little Poulton Hall for several generations, until following a marriage between the Heskeths and the Brockholes of Claughton, the name was hyphenated to Hesketh-Brockholes. Eventually the estate passed to William Fitzherbert, who adopted the Brockholes name. The Brockholes coat of arms is displayed on the prestigious River Wyre Hotel, Skippool.

REFRESHMENTS:
River House Restaurant, Skippool.
River Wyre Hotel, Skippool.
The Royal Oak Inn, Poulton.

Walk 29   **WHERE WENNING AND LUNE MEET**   3m (5km)

Maps: OS Sheets Landranger 97; Pathfinder 637.

A pleasant riverside ramble along the River Wenning to its confluence with the Lune, then upstream to Loyn Bridge.

Start: At 585685, St Margaret's Church, Hornby.

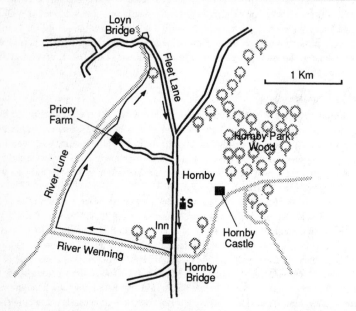

From the front the church, turn left along the road, passing the Castle Hotel on the right. Just before the bridge over the River Wenning, turn right, through a signed wicket and turn left along a flagged path to the riverside. The path turns right, downstream: follow it, continuing along a green path through woodland. Soon, the path curves to the right, climbs a few steps and turns left to reach a stile in a wall. Go over into a field and follow the path along its left edge, with a fine view back to **Hornby Castle**. Go over a stile in the field's left-hand corner and follow the left edge of the next field, still walking beside the River Wenning, on your left. Where the River Wenning flows into the Lune, simply make a right angle turn, with the path, and continue, now with the Lune on your left. The river at this point has been reinforced

62

with huge boulders which blend quite well into the background. As you walk upstream, Priory Farm is seen ahead and a little to the right.

As the river curves gently to the right, its original route, now largely dried-up, lies between the line of walk and the present riverbed, though this is quickly regained. Continue upstream, passing a succession of newly planted trees, planted to help bind together the riverbank. Where the river begins to curve to the left, and the ground ahead begins to rise, climb to the rim of the rising ground and continue edging it, for a short distance, until a cart track crosses your line of walk. Descend left, along the track, to the field corner on the left, at the riverbank. As you make the descent, Loyn Bridge can be seen ahead. At the field corner cross a step stile and continue along the riverbank on a clear path that cuts through a steep wooded bank. The path has been renovated recently, is partly stepped and very easy to follow. Soon the path climbs: it is built up in parts and stepped in others. Soon a post with a yellow arrow on it is passed, beyond which the path descends towards the river. At the end of the wood, go over a step stile. It has hardly any steps on the wood side but a lot on the other side, so care is needed when crossing. Continue underneath an arch of Loyn Bridge and immediately turn right alongside the bridge's buttress to reach stone steps. Climb these on to a cart track and turn right along it, climbing for a short distance to reach a stile to the right of a metal gate. Cross the stile on to Fleet Lane and turn left along it. On the outskirts Fleet Lane meets Moor Lane. Go right along this lane, going through the village to return to St Margaret's church.

POINTS OF INTEREST:
Hornby Castle – The neat flower bedecked village of Hornby is dominated by its castle. Occupying a site used in turn by the Romans, Horni, a Viking raider and possibly Ulf, a Danish landowner, it was built by the Norman Montbegons. Eventually it came into the possession of Edward Stanley, a stepbrother of Henry Tudor. Two of Stanley's hobbies were astronomy and alchemy causing the locals to believe that he was dabbling in black magic.

REFRESHMENTS:
The Castle Hotel, Hornby.

Walk 30   DENNY BECK AND CROOK O' LUNE   3m (5km)

Maps: OS Sheets Landranger 97; Pathfinder 637.

Riverside walking almost all the way.

Start: At 503646, Denny Beck car park.

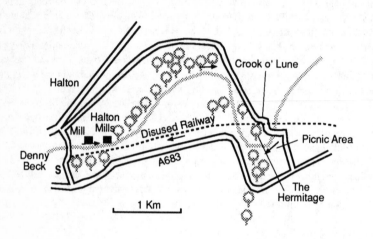

From the car park turn left, along the road, soon crossing the River Lune. Turn right, passing a lawnmower service depot. Continue along the road to reach, in a short distance, a facing gate. Go through and walk along a quiet lane, passing several buildings to reach a facing pair of gates. Cross a step stile to the right and continue along the lane, with the River Lune on your right. Just before reaching a second pair of gates, bear left, along a path that climbs slightly, then levels to contour a thickly wooded bank. Go over a step stile and continue along the path, which continues contouring the steep riverside bank. The path passes a **weir**, then continues upstream through an area which, along the bottom of a steep bank, is grassed and scattered with whins. Pass a little feeder by descending steps, crossing a plank bridge and climbing more steps. When the path reaches another wooded area a feeder is crossed on a footbridge. The path continues through trees, soon reaching a post with a yellow arrow, confirming that you are on course. The path climbs towards the top of a wooded bank to avoid very steep ground. At the top, go through a kissing gate and turn right along a footpath that edges a road.

Just before the road curves right to bridge a disused railway and the river, Crook o' Lune picnic site is passed on the left. Cross the Lune on the road bridge and turn right, using a roadside footpath. Soon, go through a kissing gate in railings on the right and follow a green path along the riverside, going through another picnic area. Continue downstream, going between beautiful trees, then cross a feeder on a footbridge. Shortly after, go over a stile into woodland. Continue along a clear path which becomes a little indistinct as it climbs and descends, through thick woodland. The path goes straight up the riverbank, through dense undergrowth towards the bank's top, then approaches a road. Turn right just a few feet from the road and follow a path along the bank top, walking parallel to the road. The path descends towards the river: it can be slippery, so care is needed. At the bottom of the bank, continue downstream, going under the lower of two railway bridges that span the river at Crook o' Lune. Soon, a stepped path is met at right angles. Turn right along it, then go over a stile on the left. Now continue down the riverside, going through thinned woodland. Once clear of the trees, go along the edge of a long field, exiting over a step stile. Stay beside the river, crossing a settlement tank (?) to reach a weir. A few yards below it, cross a step stile in a facing fence and go along a clear path. After a few yards, turn left, up steps, to reach a fork. Take the right-hand branch, climbing to continue beside, but above, the river. The path goes uphill to reach a disused railway line at right angles. Turn right and follow this to Denny Beck's old railway station. Now cross the road to return to the car park.

POINTS OF INTEREST:

Weir – There is a fish pass built into the weir to allow salmon to reach their spawning grounds.

REFRESHMENTS:

There is a Snack Bar at the Crook o' Lune picnic site.

Walk 31   SOLOMON'S TEMPLE   3m (5km)

Maps: OS Sheets Landranger 103; Pathfinder 689.

Good walking up Withnell Moor's northern flank to a failed farm.

Start: At 644244, the Hare and Hounds Inn, Abbey Village.

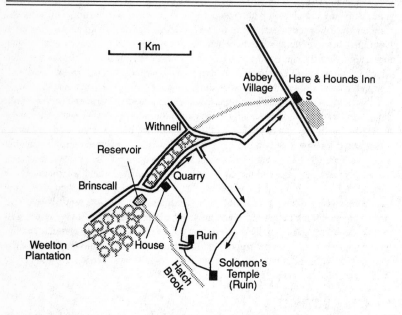

From the Inn, cross the A675, with care, and follow a roadside footpath that edges the road to Withnell. After about ¹/₂ mile the road turns sharp right and a little further on a minor road branches away, diagonally left. Follow this minor road for a short distance, then turn left up a lane with a water course to the right. When the tarmac surface ends, keep straight ahead along a track, passing a detached house on the right to reach a gate. Cross a waymarked stile to the left on to moorland and follow a track that climbs steadily through heather. After ¹/₂ mile, as a facing ruinous wall is approached, turn right along a path, following it to a gate. Go through and bear half-right along a path across the moor to reach a gateway to **Solomon's Temple**. To the right of the gateway there is a post with some yellow arrows on it. Follow the arrow pointing straight ahead, passing the ruin on the left. At the farm's far corner another arrow points half-right. Go through thistles to reach a beck close to a ruinous wall. Cross the wall and follow the beck, on your left, across a rough pasture. Go over a stile and follow an arrow on it that points downstream. Cross a bridge over a feeder and a lane, going half-right to reach a stile.

Cross the next field to reach a ruinous farm. The path passes to the left of the ruin: at its end turn right, along a walled lane. Go over a stile, turn left for a few yards, then turn left again through a gateway on to moorland. Turn right and walk beside a new fence to reach a ruinous wall. Turn left, along it, descending towards the village of Brinscall ahead. Go to the left of some ruins, keeping ahead, downhill, now following a walled lane. At the lane end, turn right, along a broad green path, which descends a bank and follows a wall to a stile. Go over and continue along the path, passing a large house, on the left, to reach a road. Go right, passing Brinscall Quarry, on the right. Soon you reach the outward route: retrace it back to the start.

POINTS OF INTEREST:

Solomon's Temple – Ruinous farms, like Solomon's Temple, scattered around the edges of Lancashire's moors, bear testament to the frugal conditions under which the 19th century farmer lived. For many, trying to make a living in such isolated and inhospitable places became just too big a burden to carry. They saw no future in farming along the moor's edge and moved away, seeking other employment, often in the thriving cotton industry, leaving their lonely farms to the elements and decay. The homes they left behind were often inadequate. Many had only small windows which could not be opened, so fresh air was unable to penetrate the cheerless rooms which could be icy cold during severe winters. Downstairs floors were of broken flags, while upstairs, wooden partitions separated the sleeping areas.

REFRESHMENTS:

The Hare and Hounds, Abbey Village.

Walk 32 SILVERDALE, HEALD BROW AND WOODWELL 3½m (5½km)

Maps: OS Sheets Landranger 97; Pathfinder 636.

A pretty walk offering extensive views across Morecombe Bay.
Start: At 458749, the car park at the west end of Shore Road,
Silverdale.

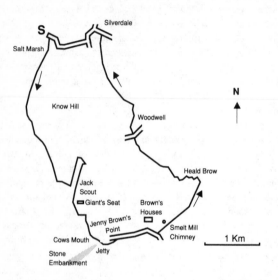

From the car park go south, keeping close to the cliffs to avoid the channels on the marsh, to Know End Point, where a notice warns of fast incoming tides. Here scramble up the rocks for about 20 feet to reach a path and continue along it, taking care because it is a bit crumbly. This is the high tide route: at low tide continue along the sands for a further 200 yards to where the path can be gained easily as it descends into a cove. The high tide route climbs to the clifftop and soon descends into another little cove to climb back to the clifftop at its other end. Now the path, much improved, continues skirting a craggy inlet and crossing a headland, to reach Cows Mouth, another inlet, passing the back of it on a path that goes past the foot of a shallow, wooded dell. Where the crags on the right diminish, take a faint path, right, to a sheep hole in a wall. Creep through it to reach Jack Scout, a National Trust heath where paths meander among the scrub. Take the path straight ahead, to a clearing containing a restored lime kiln. Bear right, over a rise, to join another track and turn left, along it, to the top edge of Cows Mouth. Over to the left is the Giant's Seat a limestone outcrop, that suits its name: go and sit on it: the views are terrific!

Descend to a path close to a fence near the shore, crossing two stiles. Continue along the path towards a road and, ignoring two gates, descend rightwards, to the head of the breakwater and the old jetty at **Jenny Brown's Point**. Continue over the rocks to reach a lane at a seat. Go right, along it, passing on your left, a long quarry and Brown's Cottages. Where the lane curves right, a prominent chimney, all that remains of a copper smelting mill, comes into view. Cross a stile on to an embankment and go left, along a path signposted 'Woodwell'. Go through a gate and take the path diagonally right, uphill. Next go diagonally left through the gorse. Go through a slit stile in a fence and continue, firstly through trees, then scrub, to reach the wooded top of Heald Brow. At a junction of paths bear right to a fence and stile on the left. Continue along a wall and go through a gap in a facing wall. Go diagonally right, past a building on your left, to reach a gate. Beyond, join a track on the left, leading to a road. Cross and take a descending path, below crags, to reach a square pool, **Woodwell**. From the adjacent car park take the path into the wood near a seat. Go through a gap in a wall and turn right along a path that soon passes a cottage on the right and continues past houses on the left and through a walled snicket to reach the main road. Turn left and go down Shore Road to the car park.

POINTS OF INTEREST:

Jenny Brown's Point – The stone embankment that runs a long way into the bay here is all the remains of an over ambitious land reclamation scheme of 1873. The intention was to reclaim the marshes between Jenny Brown's Point and Hest Bank but the company ran out of funds and the scheme was abandoned.

Woodwell – Once an important watering spot for drover's cattle.

Walk 33   HOGHTON TOWER   3¹⁄₂m (5¹⁄₂km)

Maps: OS Sheets Landranger 103; Pathfinder 689.
A fine walk centered on historical Hoghton Tower.
Start: At 624252, Finnington's Marina, Riley Green.

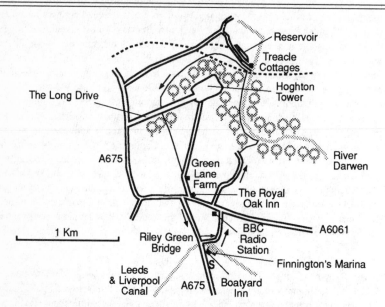

From the entrance to the Marina turn right, cross the bridge and immediately turn right through a gate and descend to the canal towpath. On reaching a 'Visitors Moorings' sign, leave the canal bank, going to the left of a fence along a descending path, which curves away from the canal and develops into a hedged lane that passes a BBC radio station, left. At the lane end turn left, briefly, along the A6061, on a roadside path. Go past a house, then turn right, with care, along a signed lane. Where this turns left into a cottage, turn right through a small gate beside a larger one. Cross a field, along a stony track, descending to cross a stile and follow a track through woodland. Where the track ends, bear left to cross a stile. Continue along a path beside the River Darwen, soon crossing a footbridge. The path continues along the riverbank into a wooded area, then passes a steep weir and broadens into a track alongside a sluice, which eventually goes underneath into the river. Continue along the track, crossing a

70

bridge over another sluice. Go under a railway viaduct and bear left, with the track, to pass Treacle Cottages. Go to the left of an old mill, then, where the track becomes surfaced, turn left up a walled lane. At the top, go over a stile continue beside the railway.

On reaching a level crossing, turn left, over the line into woodland. Go up a track, passing the remains of a bridge, then bearing right towards a wall. Turn right, along the wall, as signed, to reach a stile. Go over, leaving the wood. Walk along the wall on the left, cross a stile and continue along the wall to reach another stile. The wall now curves sharp left to another stile. Go over and keep ahead along a track, passing several cottages to reach the main approach to **Hoghton Tower**. Turn left, through a gate and go uphill to visit the tower. Now descend the drive, going through two gates, then turning left through a gate into a field. Go ahead to a T-junction of tracks and turn left, uphill, to cross a ladder stile. Go along the lane through woodland, leaving over a stile. Walk ahead, going over a stile and continuing across a field to reach a ladder stile. Go down a field to a stile in the field's left-hand corner. Follow the grassy road beyond to the Royal Oak. Cross the A6061, with care, and turn right to a T-junction. Turn left to return to the start.

POINTS OF INTEREST:

Hoghton Tower – The de Hoghton family have owned land at Hoghton since the time of William the Conqueror and in 1565 Thomas Hoghton built Hoghton Tower, the only true baronial residence in Lancashire. On August 17th, 1617, King James I, while dining at the Tower, so greatly enjoyed his loin of beef that he knighted it Sir Loin, and sirloin it remains to this day. Perhaps the most famous person associated with the minstrel's gallery, which overlooks the banqueting hall, was William Shakespeare, who performed there with Thomas Hoghton's troop of players.

REFRESHMENTS:

The Royal Oak Inn, Riley Green.
The Boatyard Inn, Riley Green.

Walk 34　　**DARWEN MOOR**　　$3^1/_2$m ($5^1/_2$km)

Maps: OS Sheets Landranger 103; Pathfinder 689.

Glorious woodland and exhilarating moorland.

Start: At 666215, the car park opposite Tockholes Nature Trail.

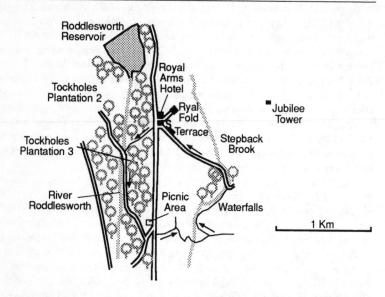

From the car park cross the road and go through a signed kissing gate into North-West Water land near Roddlesworth Reservoir. Follow a descending path through woodland, ignoring the stepped path, to the right, and a path to the left. As the path curves left it develops into a broad drive, then, as it reaches the end of the wooded area, it narrows to a path size again, all the while descending. Ignore a broad green track to the left and go right at a fork along a path that soon becomes paved with chippings. On meeting a track at right angles, turn left along it, descending through woodland to reach a gate. Go through, but do not turn right over a bridge: instead, go straight ahead along a forest track that climbs alongside the infant River Roddlesworth, on the right. Ignore all minor paths to the left and right, staying on the main track which becomes steeper. After $^1/_2$ mile the track levels out and goes through heather and thinner woods. On reaching a facing gate at a T-junction, turn left along the same broad track. Where it gains a tarmac surface, pass a picnic area on the left, continuing along what is now a surfaced road. About 20 yards short of its T-junction with a minor road, go through a gate with a Jubilee Tower marker, on the right, into a wood. Bear left along a path, as directed by a yellow arrow, keeping just inside the wood. At the next Jubilee Tower marker turn left, over a stile, on to a road. Cross it and go through a gate, also with a Jubilee Tower sign, and follow a path signed 'Lion Den: $^3/_4$ mile'.

Continue along a track on to the moor, following it to a waymarked stile beside a gateway in a facing fence. Go over and continue up the rough pasture beyond, going diagonally right at first, then turning left. Where a path heads off left, keep straight ahead, as directed by a Jubilee Tower marker. Pass a post with two yellow arrows on it, climbing and bearing slightly left. The path is very clear, meandering a little, but soon reaching a yellow arrow on a post which confirms the route. Continue along the path, climbing steeply to another waymarked post. Continue climbing to another waymarked post, this one beside a seat where you can rest. Go over the nearby stile, beside a gate in a fence and follow the path as it contours the hill before curving left and descending gently into a valley. **Jubilee Tower** can now be seen. When the path reaches another Jubilee Tower marker, turn sharp left on a path that curves right, beside trees, and edges a ghyll on the left. As it descends the path broadens into a wide track, soon reaching a stile beside a gate. Go over and follow a descending track, which curves left and edges a wall. Ignore the arches in this wall and keep ahead to cross a stile beside a gate. Now follow a fenced lane ahead, climbing through trees and going through the right-hand of two gates. Follow a track over rough pasture, leaving through a kissing gate. Now pass to the left of a terrace to return to the car park.

POINTS OF INTEREST:

Jubilee Tower – The tower was erected in 1898 to commemorate the Diamond Jubilee of Queen Victoria. An anti-clockwise spiral staircase leads to a balcony from where another climbs to the top, from where the views are very impressive.

REFRESHMENTS:

The Royal Arms Hotel, Ryal Fold.

Walk 35   HIGHER STONY BANK   3½m (5½km)

Maps: OS Sheets Landranger 103; Pathfinder 660.

A heady confection of rough pasture, field and track walking spiced with fine views of Stocks Reservoir.

Start: At 746538, Higher Stony Bank Farm.

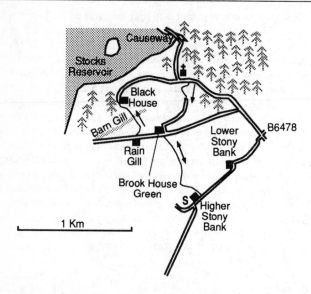

From Higher Stony Bank farm, some 2½ miles east-north-east of Slaidburn, go through a gate immediately to the east of the farmhouse and descend a steep slope through rough pasture, bearing slightly to the left at the bottom of the hill to go through a gate. Go diagonally left across the rough pasture beyond, as directed by a yellow arrow, to reach a plank bridge over a stream. Cross and go diagonally right to reach a stile in a wall. Go over and cross the next rough pasture, bearing slightly right to keep to the left side of what looks like a deep drain. Soon a farm, Brook House Green, comes into view. Aim for it, leaving the field over a stile. Turn left, along the farm road. This soon develops a tarmac surface, goes through a gateway and continues, climbing steadily. It then loses its tarmac surface as it descends to Rain Gill Farm. On approaching the first building on the left, go over a concrete bridge on the right and through a gate. Cross a field along a green track that curves to the right. On reaching a facing gate do not go through: instead, turn left, as directed by a yellow arrow, and follow the wall on the right. At the bottom of the field go past another waymarker, over a concrete bridge and cross a stile into a meadow. Go straight up the centre of the meadow, along a shallow depression, walking parallel to the wall on the right. Go through a gate and cross the next field diagonally left towards Black House Farm.

Go through a gate into the farmyard and turn left, between farm buildings. Now turn right to go through a gate at the end of the building on the right and continue forward at the other end of the building to follow a farm road, right, in front of the farm. On leaving the farm, in the valley bottom on the left, Stocks Reservoir can be seen. Follow the farm road through a gate to join a road, just to the right of **St James' Church**. Continue along the road, going uphill through woodland. Where the road curves right, turn right along a signed path. Continue through woodland, following the path as it descends and gradually curves right to reach a stile. Go over, but after about four yards cross another stile in a facing wall. Now go diagonally left, across a meadow, aiming for a gate in front of a farm building. Soon a facing gate is reached: go through, and follow a track which curves to the right and then edges a narrow valley on the right. After a while the track turns left, away from the valley, and curves right to reach the left-hand side of Brook House Green Farm. Turn left along the farm road for a few yards to where it meets another farm road at a tangent. Now turn right along that road for a few yards to the point where you joined it on the outward leg and turn left, up a bank, to cross a stile in a facing wall. From here retrace your steps across rough pasture, back to Higher Stony Bank Farm.

POINTS OF INTEREST:

St James' Church – This isolated church in the parish of Stocks-in-Bowland, is the head church of the valley. A notice in the churchyard invites people to 'pause awhile and rest'. This is sound advice because it is a lovely church with an interesting past.

REFRESHMENTS:
None on the walk, but available in nearby Slaidburn.

Walk 36   SAMLESBURY   3¹/₂m (5¹/₂km)

Maps: OS Sheets Landranger 102; Pathfinder 679 and 680.
A gentle, historical walk along quiet lanes and fields.
Start: At 591302, Church Bottoms.

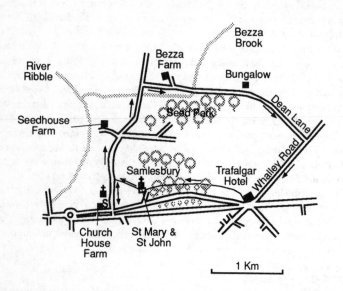

From the entrance to Church House farm at the south end of Potter Lane, go northwards along the lane, passing the church of **St Leonard's-the-Less** on the left. A little further along the lane, just past the entrance to a nursery on the left, go straight ahead along a road prohibited to motor vehicles. Soon Seedhouse Farm is passed on the left. Cross Bezza Brook, walk past a house on the right, and turn right at a junction to continue along Dean Lane, edged for a while with a lovely beech hedge which attempts to hide a large manicured lawn. Pass 'Buttonoak' on the right, then, where the lane curves sharp left towards Bezza Park Farm, turn right along a grassy lane which is a continuation of Dean Lane.

Soon you cross Bezza Brook again, continuing straight ahead, just inside the woodland of Seed Park. The lane climbs steadily at first, then more steeply. Eventually the climb becomes less severe and almost at the top of the rise a lovely bungalow is seen a field away on the left. The way ahead is now much more open, the lane much less cluttered. Soon, a T-junction is reached. Turn right along Whalley Road, using a roadside footpath. On reaching a busy road junction, keep on the footpath, which passes in front of the Trafalgar Hotel, on the right, and continues along Preston New Road, still on the footpath. Just past the hotel, and short of a bus stop, turn right, over a stile, and go along a lane. In a short distance there is a gateway in the hedge on the right. Do not go through: instead, keep straight ahead, crossing a field close to the hedge on the right to reach a stile in the right-hand corner of the field.

Go over and keep ahead along the left-hand side of the field, beside an overgrown sunken lane, to go over a stile in a facing hedge. Continue ahead to reach, and go alongside, a hawthorn hedge on the right, heading towards trees. When there is a step in the hedge on the right, a lane that bears away to the right can be seen ahead. Continue down this lane, soon crossing a stile to reach a sunken track. Keep ahead, just inside a narrow wood, to exit into the grounds of a **Roman Catholic Church**. Continue straight ahead, passing the church hall on the right, and then turn right at the far end of the **Presbytery garden**. Go along a short lane to re-enter a field through a gate. Go downhill, close to the hedge on the left, leaving the field through a gateway at the left-hand corner of a facing hedge on to the lane used on the outward leg. Turn left to return to the start.

POINTS OF INTEREST:

St Leonard's-the-Less – A witches grave, funerary armour and box pews are all found here, together with a letter dated 1685 which requests permission to teach a few children in the chapel because the schoolmaster's cottage was very small and smokey.

Roman Catholic Church – The church of St Mary and St John Southworth contains a shrine to St John Southworth. Timber from the old staircase at Lower Hall, less than a mile away to the north, alongside the River Ribble, was fashioned into the Sanctuary Cross.

Presbytery garden – The view from the gate near the garden embraces the Ribble Valley flood plain which, so legend has it, was dedicated to St Leonard. A string of churches along the river's length dedicated to St Leonard would appear to bear this out.

REFRESHMENTS:

The Trafalgar Hotel, at the Preston New Road/Whalley Road junction.

Walk 37 THORNTON LODGE AND COCKLE HALL $3^1/_2$m ($5^1/_2$km)

Maps: OS Sheets Landranger 102; Pathfinder 658.

Wonderful Wyre estuary walking with lots of birdlife.

Start: At 355406, Thornton Lodge, Skippool.

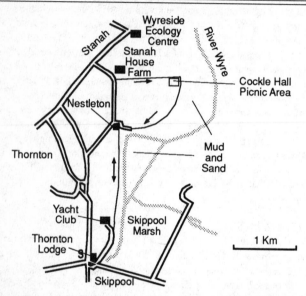

From Thornton Lodge, which stands at the south end of Wyre Road, where it meets the A585(T) at a roundabout on Skippool's northern edge, go northwards along Wyre Road, using a roadside footpath, edging Skippool Creek on the right. Where the road curves slightly to the left, walk ahead along a track, passing to the right of the **Fleetwood and Blackpool Yacht Club**. Now follow a clear estuary path, passing, on the right, a whole string of moorings. Just past the last of these, at a signpost 'To Underbank Road, 200 yards' turn left and go through a small gate, to the side of a larger one, into a lane. Follow the lane to a facing road. Turn right, along the road (Underbank Road). Soon after passing Oakland Cottage, on the left, and before reaching Stanah House Farm, turn right, go over a stile into a field on a signed path for Cockle Hall. Follow a field track – which curves slightly left, and continues beside a hedge on the right – guided by a yellow arrow. Where the hedge on the right ends, go straight ahead, as directed by another yellow arrow on a post. Go under a line of electricity towers and continue to reach two facing gateways. Go through the left-hand one, as directed by two arrows on a post, and walk beside a line of gorse bushes on the right, crossing climbing ground which offers good views of the estuary and Fleetwood on the left.

The field climbs quite steeply – you are climbing over a drumlin (*see* Note to Walk 13) – and at its brow a yellow arrow points straight ahead, downhill. Stay close to a hedge on the right to reach a step stile in the right-hand corner of a facing fence. Go over and follow a path between small trees to reach a facing footpath, the Wyre Way. Turn right along this, passing Cockle Hall picnic area (*see* Note to Walk 13). Continue along the path, which edges the saltmarshes offering fine views of the rich birdlife they support. On reaching the signpost from where you turned left, through a gate, on the outward leg, turn left and retrace your steps back to Thornton Lodge.

POINTS OF INTEREST:

The Blackpool and Fleetwood Yacht Club – The club is based at Skippool and frequently holds competitions on the river. Always navigable, in recent years the Wyre has become increasingly used as a base for leisure craft. Many people enjoy sailing on the river because it is so calm. An old saying 'Safe and easy as Wyre water' is an apt one. Yet the estuary can be dangerous because conditions can change dramatically with the tide. Sailing at low tide is almost impossible and carries an element of danger. In fact, sailing there is safe for only a couple of hours after high tide. However, when the tide is good and high on a fine Sunday afternoon, the estuary is alive with activity because, as Rat pointed out, *there is nothing – absolutely nothing – half as much worth doing as simply messing about in boats*.

REFRESHMENTS:
Thornton Lodge, Skippool.
River Wyre Hotel, Skippool.

Walk 38   BLACKO AND ALKINCOATS   4m (6½km)

Maps: OS Landranger 103; Pathfinder 670.
A walk over fields to a canal.
Start: At 860415, Blacko School.

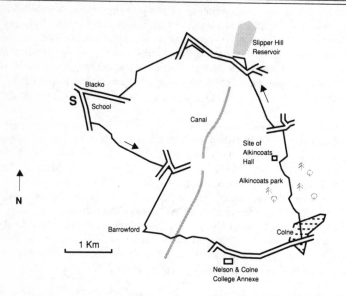

From the school go down Gisburn Road to the Rising Sun and turn left along a track between houses. At the end of the buildings cross a stile on your right, go uphill and over a stile into a lane. Turn left and, where the lane turns sharp left, go through the middle of three stiles. Go ahead, over two more stiles, to reach a third one in a field corner. Go down the next field, close to a wall on your right. Ignoring the opening on your right, keep to the left of a building to reach a road. Cross towards a facing path, but do not go along it. Instead, take the path to the right, going diagonally over a field to a stile. Beyond the stile the path continues straight ahead, parallel to a road on the right and keeping to the left of an overgrown area. At the bottom of the path turn right to a kissing gate and go forward to a corner opening which leads to Grange Avenue. Turn left at the bottom of it to reach another kissing gate, and cross the field ahead to the lock-keepers's cottage. Cross the canal on a footbridge, turn right on the towpath, cross a stile on your left and follow a field path towards the Nelson and Colne College Annex. On reaching the road, turn left for about 300 yards to where, at the first street, you turn left into Alkincoats Park. Go through the park towards its top left corner, keeping to the right of ruinous Alkincoats Hall. Leave the Park through a kissing gate and go along a track to reach Red Lane. Cross, go over a stile and take a path through a quarry heading for Blacko Tower and crossing stiles to reach a road. Go along the road going over the course of an old railway line, then over a stream, with the entrance to Foulridge Tunnel below and to your left. Go over a stile on the right, uphill, to the side of Slipper Hill Reservoir, continuing clockwise along its bank to a stile leading back to the road. Go up the road as far as a house on the right and there go left, through a gap in the wall; Cross a stream and on to reach a stile in the field ahead. Turn right, uphill, to a stile near a gate leading to a road. Cross, and turn left, briefly, to where a path forks right. The path crosses several stiled fields and turns left when alongside a farm. Follow a fence to a gate on the left, go through and turn right. Follow a hedge and a fence to Beverley Road and turn right, along it, back to the school.

REFRESHMENTS:
The Rising Sun Inn, Blacko.

Walk 39   CHIPPING AND LOUD MYTHAM   4m (6½km)

Maps: OS Sheets Landranger 103; Pathfinder 669.

Through quiet farmland and along the river Loud.

Start: At 624432, Prapins Endowed Primary School, Chipping.

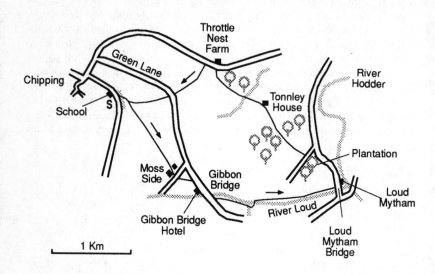

Turn right along the road, and soon after it leaves Chipping and curves right, turn left to cross a stream. Continue close to a fence on the left, and at a field corner turn right, briefly, to cross a stile in the fence on the left. Cross the field beyond, bearing slightly right towards a hawthorn in a line of trees about 100 yards right of a fence. Just beyond the hawthorn cross a marshy stream and keep ahead, aiming for the right side of some huts ahead. Go over a stile and walk past the huts, on the left, and a building, on the right, continuing along an unsurfaced lane. At its end, cross a facing lane and go over a stile into a field. Cross, bearing slightly left to reach a stile midway along a facing fence. Go over and cross a field, bearing slightly left towards its left-hand corner to reach a waymarked stile. Go over and turn right along a road, passing the Gibbon Bridge Hotel. Cross a bridge over the River Loud and immediately turn left through a tiny gate. Descend a ladder into a field. Cross, close to the river, to a stile.

Go over and continue downstream. On approaching a feeder, keep to the high ground on the right, soon crossing it by footbridge. Immediately turn left, towards the River Loud, crossing it on stepping stones. Cross a stile and turn right to climb a bank to a stile into a field. Go downstream, now with the river on your right. Go over a stile and continue along the river, leaving the field over a stile. Cross a ditch and follow the river, but after a short distance take a path along a wooded embankment. Beyond, leave the field over a stile on to a road some 25 yards left of where Loud Mytham Bridge spans the river. Turn left, uphill, along the road which continues along an embankment with the Hodder below, on the right. Where the road turns sharp right, keep ahead, as signed, through the right-hand of two gates. Cross the field beyond diagonally right to join the fence on the left, which at one point curves left. The fence is rejoined at a corner: maintain direction towards the field's right-hand corner. On approaching it you will see a thin plantation intruding on the right.

Cross a stile at the right-hand end of this plantation, go to the left of a pool, and exit over a stile on to a farm road. Cross this and the large field ahead, aiming towards its left-hand corner where the fence on the left meets, at right angles, a facing line of trees. Continue parallel to a wood on the left, heading towards Tonnley House. Go through a gate to the left of the house, then bear left across a field to ford a stream just downstream of a collapsed footbridge. The footbridge is signposted and easily seen. Go forward, then bear left and go through a gate in the fence on your left. Cross a field, staying close to the fence on the right to where it starts to edge a wood. There, go diagonally left, crossing the field corner to reach a stile in a facing fence. Go over and cross the next field on rising ground, bearing right to cross a signed stile in its right-hand corner on to a road. Turn left, uphill, passing Throstle Nest Farm on the right. Where the road curves right, turn left through a gate and walk along an unsurfaced track, soon reaching Dairy Barn Farm. Continue past it, following a concrete road and, at its far end, go diagonally left across a road. Cross a waymarked stile on to a rough pasture, continuing close to the hedge on the right. Cross a ruinous stile about 10 yards from the field's right-hand corner and continue over the next rough pasture, still staying close to the fence on the right. On approaching the next facing fence, go slightly left to cross it at a stile used on the outward leg. Now retrace your steps to Chipping.

REFRESHMENTS:
The Sun Inn, Chipping.

Walk 40   LADY HAMILTON'S WELL   4m (6$\frac{1}{2}$km)

Maps: OS Sheets Landranger 102; Pathfinder 668.

The Pilling Pig and a woman with a diabolical temper.

Start: At 494454, the car park at Garstang Community Centre.

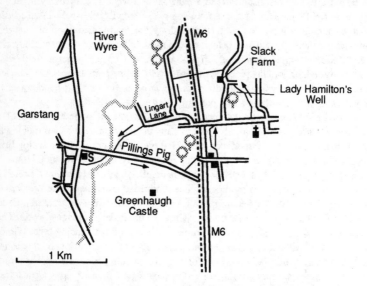

From the car park, to the west of the River Wyre, go upstream, along the riverbank, soon passing a sports field on your left. On reaching a concrete bridge, climb steps to reach **Pilling Pig**, the track bed of the former Garstang and Knott End railway. Turn right, cross the River Wyre, and walk along the old track, crossing four stiles. To the right is **Greenhaigh Castle**. After about $\frac{1}{2}$ mile, a cutting is reached. Do not enter: instead, climb the bank on the left and cross a stile. Go diagonally right across the field beyond, passing a solitary tree and passing Castle Wood, on the left, to exit over a ladder stile. Walk ahead, crossing bridges over the Euston to Glasgow railway and the M6. Now, just short of a house dated 1730, turn left and go past a farm on the left into a field. Bear left to a fence that edges the M6 and continue beside it to cross two closely spaced stiles. Go diagonally right across the field beyond, close to a hedge/fence that runs beside a stream. Go over a stile on to a road and turn right along it for

600 yards to reach a red postbox just short of Barnacre Church. There, turn left down steps and cross a stream on a wooden footbridge.

Turn left, soon crossing a stile in a facing fence. Go diagonally right, uphill, across the field beyond, keeping to the right of a disused quarry before descending to walk beside a wood on the left. Cross a stile, beyond which, on the right, among bushes are the remains of **Lady Hamilton's Well**. From the well go diagonally right across a field to reach a stile on to a farm track. Turn left, briefly, to reach a T-junction with Keeper's Lane. Turn right, passing Slack Farm, on the left. Soon after, turn left over a stile into a field. Cross this, staying close to the hedge on your right, but where this ends, keep straight ahead to re-cross the M6 and the railway line. Go straight ahead across a field to reach Hazelhead Lane. Turn left, but where the lane turns sharp left, turn right along Lingart Lane, an unsurfaced farm track. Where the track makes a sharp turn right, cross a stile on the left and follow a footpath across two fields, going over three stiles to rejoin the disused railway track used on the outward leg. Turn right and retrace your steps to the car park.

POINTS OF INTEREST:

Pilling Pig – This section of the former Garsdale to Knott End Railway, which was opened on 5th December 1870, and closed in 1963, was known at the Pilling Pig because an engine, called the Farmer's Friend, purchased for use on the line in 1876 had a whistle that sounded like a dying pig. Although the engine was sold in 1883, the name stuck, becoming associated with the line itself rather than the engine.

Greenhaigh Castle – A ruinous tower is all that remains of the castle, which was built in 1490. A Royalist stronghold in the Civil War, it withstood a two year siege before surrendering in 1645. It has been ruinous since 1649.

Lady Hamilton's Well – Lady Hamilton of Ashton Hall and her husband, the Duke, spent several months of the year at Woodacre Hall from where she would frequently come to the well to drink its water, which was supposed to possess healing properties. A pillar of both church and establishment, Lady Hamilton was a handsome lady with a ready wit but, according to Dean Swift, a 'diabolical temper'. On one occasion this formidable lady drove the Garsdale Independents out of their chapel by threatening to horsewhip them.

REFRESHMENTS:

There are numerous possibilities in Garstang.

Walk 41   **LEIGHTON MOSS**   4m (6¹/₂km)

Maps: OS Sheets Landranger 97; Pathfinder 636.
A Nature Reserve, Leighton Hall and magnificent scenery.
Start: At 475752, Silverdale railway station.

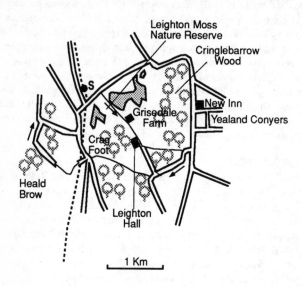

From the railway station turn left, along the road to a road junction. Turn left for about a ¹/₄ mile, then turn right along a bridleway to cross **Leighton Moss Nature Reserve** along an impressive ¹/₂ mile long causeway, passing a bird hide. Leave the causeway through a gate into a field and follow a climbing track to Grizedale Farm. Go through the farmyard and go up a lane. Go past an old coach house, on the right, and continue through parkland to **Leighton Hall**. Leave the Hall along its drive but, after 50 yards, bear left, going uphill on grass and keeping to the right of a fenced enclosure. A seat on the hill's summit offers a panoramic view across Morecombe Bay to the Lakeland Fells.

    Continue through a kissing gate and maintain direction across a field, passing a stone mound and descending through trees on a path which goes through a gap stile on to a road. Here a short detour left into Yealand Conyers is advised because at the north end of the village the New Inn provides bar meals and refreshments. The walk, however, turns right at the gap stile, going along a road which passes between pleasantly wooded pastures. Soon after passing the entrance to Leighton Hall, on the right, the road curves left: just beyond this bend turn right along an unsurfaced lane, exiting through a gate into a field. Cross this close to the wall on the right. At first the way is indistinct, but it quickly improves. Just before the path curves left, leave it, bearing right, downhill, to go over a gap stile. Continue along the downhill path beyond, going through trees to more open ground where, at a large oak, a footpath sign confirms your route. Keep descending gently to exit through a gate in the field's left-hand corner. Now go along the right-hand side of a field for about 500 yards to reach a gate. Go through and follow a gated track to reach a road at Crag Foot.

Here there is a choice of routes. For a short return turn right along the road for $^3/_4$ mile. Alternatively turn right , but after 200 yards turn left at a 'Silverdale' signpost, going along a track which passes under the railway. Turn right over a dyke, go through a gate and cross fields on a path, which soon goes along an embankment. At its end, go through a gate and continue along a path signed for 'Woodwell'. This climbs steeply, then bears right in front of some gorse bushes. Now bear left, following waymarkers, to a gap stile. Continue through woodland, as directed by a waymarker, to a stile. Go over and cross a field. Go diagonally right across the next field, continuing along a field track and a signposted path to reach a road. Turn right back to Silverdale Station.

POINTS OF INTEREST:
Leighton Moss Nature Reserve – Open throughout the year from 9am until 9pm, except on Tuesdays, this RSPB Reserve supports some 80 species of breeding birds, including the rare bittern, bearded tit, and marsh harrier. The reserve, which spreads over 6,540 acres, is an important stopping point for passing wildfowl and waders, and an important spot for wintering birds. It is also home to several pairs of otters. There is an RSPB Visitor Centre and hides are sited along its two miles of viewing paths.
Leighton Hall – The Gillow family, famed for their furniture making, lived in this castellated, limestone hall. The gardens include a maze and, weather permitting, during the summer months, at 3.30pm daily, there is a spectacular flying display of eagles and other birds of prey. There is a tea room and gift shop.

REFRESHMENTS:
The New Inn, Yealand Conyers.
The Tea Room and Gift Shop, Leighton Hall.

Walk 42   **CARNFORTH AND BOLTON-LE-SANDS**   4m (6¹/₂km)
Maps: OS Sheets Landranger 97; Pathfinder 648 and 637.
The Lancaster Canal, fields and woodland.
Start: At 497703, Carnforth railway station.

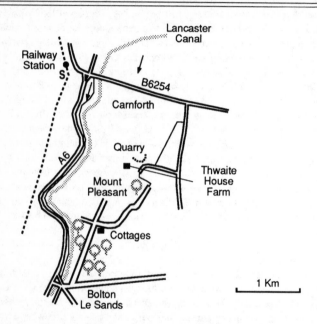

From the station turn right along Market Street to the A6. Cross, with care, and go along the B6254. Just before it bridges the **Lancaster Canal**, go right along a path down to the towpath. Turn right, southwards, for 2 miles of pleasant canal side walking. The going is easy as there are no locks, and there are usually houseboats on the water. The canal bridges are numbered: when No. 123 is reached, go under and turn right, up steps, to a road. Turn right, over the canal, into Bolton-le-Sands. Turn left, briefly, along Bolton Lane, then go left again, along Mount Pleasant Lane. The lane climbs steadily and offers good views of the canal and village set against the sandy background of Morecombe Bay. On reaching a cross-roads, turn right along a lane soon passing cottages, on the right. A little further on the lane deteriorates to a track, then narrows. Continue along the track, which is muddy, but becomes less muddy and broader as it passes mixed woodland, on the left. Beyond this the track turns left, then right. Here, Thwaite House Farm is passed on the left.

The track curves right and reaches a quarry. In a short distance go left, entering a field at its left-hand corner. Cross diagonally right, along a path, at first aiming for the right-hand side of a step in the field's left-hand boundary. Now continue, bearing more to the right to exit the field at the middle of a facing fence. Cross the field beyond, going diagonally right to exit at its right-hand corner. Cross another field, a narrow one, to reach Back Lane. Turn left along it, now with Carnforth on your left, to its junction with the B6254. Turn left to return to the railway station, perhaps taking time to visit **Steamtown**.

POINTS OF INTEREST:

Lancaster Canal – Opened in 1798, the 41 miles long Lancaster Canal is the longest lock-free length of canal in England. At one time most of the barges plying their trade along it were those carrying sand and gravel. These days it is mostly colourful houseboats, which add greatly to the canal's charm. The canal extends northwards from Preston and is navigable as far as the Tewetfield locks. Managed by the British Waterways Board, this often peaceful and picturesque canal is rich in birdlife which attracts a great many ornithologists as well as walkers.

Steamtown – The golden age of railway steam is brilliantly evoked at Carnforth's Steamtown, an ever popular visitor's attraction. Here, would be engine drivers can live out their footplate fantasies and dream of the time when Carnforth station was a busy junction through which iron monsters thundered, puffing white smoke and hissing steam.

Crawstone Wood – The wood spreads along the sloping eastern side of the Lancaster Canal, opposite the northern end of Bolton-le-Sands and can be clearly seen from the canal towpath. It, and nearby Thwaite Brow, are owned by Bolton-le-Sands Parish Council and managed through a Community Woodlands Project. There is a circular walk through the wood, which comprises beech, oak and ash.

REFRESHMENTS:

The Packet Boat Inn, Bolton-le-Sands.
There are many possibilities in Carnforth.

WYCOLLER COUNTRY PARK 4m (6¹/₂km)

Maps: OS Sheets Landranger 103; Outdoor Leisure 21.

An interesting exploration of a working hill farm.

Start: At 938394, Haworth Road car park.

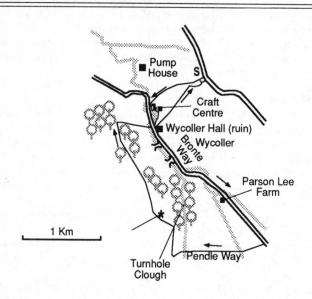

Go eastwards from the car park's north-west corner, crossing a field to reach a ladder stile. Maintain direction, joining another path and continuing along it to reach a crossroads of paths. Turn left, passing two cottages and Pepper Hill Barn, now a craft centre. When **Wycoller Beck** is reached, walk with it on your right. Soon, a pack horse bridge: continue along a road, the Bronte Way, passing the remains of Wycoller Hall, on the left, and a clapper bridge, on the right, to reach a 17th century aisled barn, now an Information Centre. Continue along Wycoller Dene, passing the single-arched Copy House Bridge and then a clam bridge, a single slab of gritstone laid across the beck. Stay on the road, passing Parsons Lee Farm on the right. Continue beside Smithy Clough, climbing on to moorland to reach a path (on the Pendle Way) on the right. Turn right along the path. Ignore a path on the right to Dean House Farm, staying on the Pendle Way, close to a wall on your left. Where the wall curves sharply left, turn

90

right to cross a stream. Follow the path across the edge of Flake Hill Moor, aiming for the left-hand corner of Turnhole Clough.

Where the path splits, take the left-hand branch, skirting Viewpoint Rocks. The path splits again: take the left-hand branch, exiting the rough pasture at a facing wall and edging more rough pasture, easing towards the wall on your right. The path comes close to woodland on the right, then curves left to cross a nature conservation area into woodland. Beyond, the path curves right to join another path. Continue down the walled lane to reach the clapper bridge. Cross, turn left, briefly, to the packhorse bridge. Turn right along a path which passes to the left of Wycoller Hall to meet another path from the right. Keep ahead, along the route of an old coach road to reach the ladder stile crossed on the outward leg. Now retrace your steps back to the car park.

POINTS OF INTEREST:

Wycoller Beck – The Anglo-Saxons had a settlement here, naming it *Wic Alr, the dairy farm among alders*. During the 1890's, when the manufacture of woollens and worsted on handlooms became an important industry, a scheme to create a reservoir by flooding Wycoller Beck was proposed, but later abandoned in favour of a borehole over which the Pump House was built. Lancashire County Council purchased the land in 1973: the village was declared a conservation area and 350 acres of the surrounding farmland was designated a Country Park.

REFRESHMENTS:

None on the route. Please bring your own and use the pleasant picnic areas.

STANAH TO SKIPPOOL 4m (6½km)
or 8m (13km)

Maps: OS Sheets Landranger 102; Pathfinder 658.
An excellent, and exciting, estuary walk.
Start: At 355432, Wyreside Ecology Centre, Stanah.

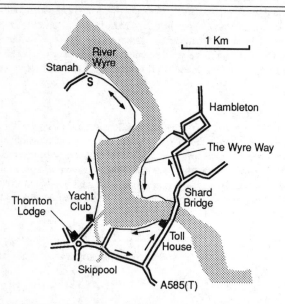

From the Centre, in **Wyre Estuary Country Park**, go half-left, across the car park, towards the estuary to join the Wyre Way (waymarked by a black arrow on a yellow background) as it curves to the right and heads southwards beside the estuary. The path is flooded sometimes, at high tide, so please take care: but don't be put off – the walk is a delight, particularly for bird lovers. The path edges saltings, then passes a picnic area. It then curves right, edging a bulge. As this is rounded, moorings are seen ahead and to the left. At a path junction, turn left, over a feeder, and continue, soon passing the moorings. Where the path ends, walk ahead, along Skippool Creek, on a road towards the A585(T). When this is seen ahead, a thin path (the Wyre Way) goes left to edge the creek. Go over a stile on to a roadside path at a roundabout on the A585, with **Skippool** beyond it.

The shorter route returns to Stanah from here: turn right along the path, then right again at a sign 'To Skippool Creek', with Thornton Lodge on the left, set back from the road. You are now walking along a path beside Wyre Road. From here, retrace your steps back to Stanah.

The longer walk turns left along the roadside path at the roundabout, following it through a residential area, then turning left along the A588. Cross the spectacular Shard Bridge, then go around left and right bends to reach a T-junction. Turn left along Shard Lane. The lane bears right, then swing left to edge Hambleton. Now, where it curves right, between dwellings, go left along a lane to reach the foreshore. There, turn left along the Wyre Way, edging the salt marshes all the way back to Shard Bridge. Cross and turn right at the Toll House on the south bank to edge the Wyre to Skippool Marsh, still following the Wyre Way. Now turn left, back to the A585. Here turn right and retrace your steps to the roundabout to rejoin the shorter route for the return to Stanah.

POINTS OF INTEREST:

The Wyre Estuary Country Park – The Park comprises the whole estuary from the river mouth to Shard Bridge. A network of paths leads walkers through a variety of habitats, allowing them to explore and discover the area's varied attractions and landscapes. The Wyreside Ecology Centre, a multi-purpose building at the Park's car park, provides information for locals and visitors alike and houses displays of the history and natural history of the area.

Skippool – Before the development of Fleetwood in the mid-1800's Skippool, the old port of Poulton-le-Fylde, was the main destination for large seafaring ships from all over the world.

REFRESHMENTS:

Thornton Lodge, Skippool.
The Farm House Kitchen, Stanah.

Maps: OS Sheets Landranger 102; Pathfinder 658.
Walking near the unspoilt marshes of Barnaby's Sand.
Start: At 346484, the Ferry Pier, Knott End.

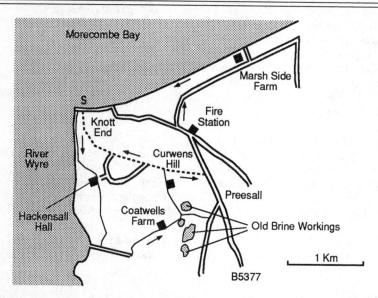

Go southwards along the waymarked Wyre Way, soon reaching Sea Dyke Cottage on your left. Turn left, then, just past the house, turn right along a track that edges a golf course. After about ⅓ mile, go half-left, across the course, aiming for the near side of buildings sited in front of the trees that surround **Hackensall Hall**. On reaching a shed, go along a track, passing farm buildings to reach a track junction. Turn left, between a wood and outbuildings, and turn left at the house. Just past a garden, turn right along a track that crosses the golf course, passing a wood on the right. Further to the right from here are **Barnaby's Sands**. Another track is reached (at a bend in it, beneath overhead wires): leave the Wyre Way, going left, along a track close to a hedge on the left. When the hedge approaches a road, go left across a field to reach a gate. Go beneath overhead wires, beside the hedge on your right, but where this turns right, bear left towards Coat Wall Farm. Join a farm track coming in from the right, following it to the farmyard. Turn right to leave the farm along a track, staying on it until it turns left. There, keep ahead, across the next field, walking parallel to the hedge on your left to reach a gate. Cross the next field, close to the fence on your right, to go through a gate on to a track. Turn left to reach Curwens Hill Farm. Go through the farmyard and left of the farmhouse to reach a stile. Go over and cross the field beyond to reach a kissing gate on to the trackbed of the disused Garstang-Knott End Railway.

The shorter route turns left here. Follow the trackbed, ignoring side tracks until a fence blocks your way. Go right, around a bungalow, and turn right along Hackensall Road to reach a seat. Turn left along a path to a road. Turn right, then left, into Parkway. Now go right, down Holmfield Road. Turn left into Quail Holme Road and follow it back to the Ferry Pier.

The longer walk turns right along the trackbed. After 600 yards, go half-left to reach a road (the B5377). Turn left, edging the eastern end of Knott End on the right. After a further 600 yards a road joins at a tangent and, beyond, a fire station is passed on the right. Continue for 400 yards, then turn right along Pilling Lane. Follow it for about a mile, to just beyond Marsh Side Farm on the left. Now, short of where the road turns sharp right, go left, along a lane to the sea front. Turn left and follow the front back to the start.

POINTS OF INTEREST:
Hackensall Hall – Built in 1656 by Richard and Anne Fleetwood of Rossall, Hackensall Hall was restored in the 19th century by Sir James Bourne. It is said that two skeletons were discovered when walls were taken down, and the hall is reported to be haunted by a horse.

Barnaby's Sands – These saltmarshes have been designated a Site of Special Scientific Interest and, together with another SSSI, Burrows Marsh, are now managed as Nature Reserves by the Lancashire Wildlife Trust. Some of the more interesting plants found at the site are glasswort, sea aster, sea lavender, sea purslane and sea wormwood. Some of the plants produce huge amounts of seed that provide winter food for wildfowl and finches, which in turn attract birds of prey. Under the mud of the estuary there is a wealth of food for waders, the equal, in energy terms, of 15 Mars Bars for every square metre.

REFRESHMENTS:
The Bourne Arms, Knott End-on-Sea.

Walk 48   BLACKO AND THE PASTURE HOUSE $4\frac{1}{2}$m (7km)

Maps: OS Landranger 103; Pathfinder 670.

The walk with a fine ridge, offering views of Nelson and Pendle.

Start: At 860415, Blacko School.

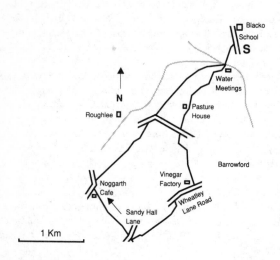

From the school cross the Gisburn Road, go downhill, and through the first kissing gate on the right. Continue over the field to a stile on the left. Cross and go along the left side of the field now facing you, aiming for a stile in a small piece of wall. Continue over another stile next to a gate to reach the riverbank. There go left at first, then cross the river on a bridge, and continue past Water Meetings Farm. Beyond, go through a stile on the left, then right, uphill, heading for a stile in a section of wall in front of a tree in the field's top corner. Continue up the hill and, as it levels, keep to the right, seeking a stile in the corner of the next field among some trees. Keep going in the same direction over several fields, soon seeing **Pasture House** ahead. Now aim for a stile on the left, hidden behind some farm buildings, which leads to a road in front of the house. Pass the house, and just beyond where the road turns left, cross a stile on the right and follow a path across a field in front of some cottages, into a cobbled lane. Here follow a Pendle Way sign past a barn, across a road and along a lane past some houses. Cross a stile on the left, when the lane turns right and follow the stream down the field to a section of wall. Ignoring the stile ahead, go right, over a stile and cross the next field to another stile. Go over and follow the path to Wheatley Lane Road. Turn right, along it, to a lane between Oakbank and Willow Bank. Go left, along the lane. Go over a stile to the left of a gate and head towards the right corner of the field where a stile leads to a path parallel to the road you have just left. Cross several fields and pass Laund Farm. On approaching a large house the path goes through a wall and eventually along a lane to Carr Hall Road. Turn right, along it to a T-junction. Keep straight ahead into Sandy Hall Lane, and follow it to its far end. Take the left of two stiles opposite Noggarth Cafe, and follow a path along a wall Soon a track joins from the left: keep going in the same direction, using the track, as far as a road going downhill to the left. Cross this, go through a stile and continue along the wall side, passing a Pendle Waymarker. On reaching the brow of a hill, look for a stile on the right. Go over and follow a path into a wood and continue through it until the Water Meetings bridge is seen again. Cross a field to the bridge, leaving it by a stile next to the bridge. Retrace your steps to Blacko School.

POINTS OF INTEREST:

Pasture House – When the house was built by the Shackleton's in 1777, Elizabeth Shackleton kept a diary and from it the progress of the building can be traced from the first plans in 1776 to when she moved in, in January, 1778.

REFRESHMENTS:

Noggarth Café at the apex of the walk.
The Rising Sun Inn, Blacko.

Walk 49 PLAIN QUARRY AND HUTTON ROOF CRAGS 4¹/₂m (7km)

Maps: OS Landranger 97; Pathfinder 637.

A fine circuit of part of Hutton Roof Crags, with a good mix of woodland a fell walking.

Start: At 555762, Plain Quarry car park.

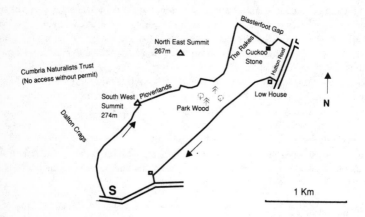

From the car park, two miles from Burton on the Whittington Road, take a path northwards from the quarry edge, bearing left into woods for 50 yards. Soon another path comes in from the left: climb on to a rocky shelf. Continue into a thicket to join another track, turn right, along it, and fork left almost at once. Here, spreading branches transform the walk into a tunnel-like avenue, with a clearing where the path swings right. The path reaches a stile in a fence at the end of the wood, leading to open fell. Go right for 30 yards, over a wall stile on your left and continue straight ahead for 100 yards, crossing open fell to a trig point marking the South-West Summit of Hutton Roof Crags – at 274 metres, a fine viewpoint. Continue NE along a cairned, grassy ridge called Ploverlands, to its far end, where it falls to a scrab-dotted limestone pavement. From the end of the ridge, bear right to a wall edging the top end of a wood, and follow a faint track that snakes between clints and shrubs. The track leaves the wall to enter a small valley, but soon returns to the wall and stays close to it as it descends. On approaching the end of the wood on your right, the path bears left, up a grassy slope and along the bottom of the Rakes, a popular practice ground for rock climbers. Beyond a little depression at its head, where paths cross, go right, through a rocky gap, and follow a path descending through more rocky gaps between great slabs of limestone. The path drops steeply past the Cuckoo Stone, a large boulder balanced precariously on a small base, into Hutton Roof village, going left, then right to a gate and along a short lane to join the village road. Turn right through the village, and turn right along a path signposted 'Crag House', through piles of junk at Low House. Beyond this the path becomes pleasant, entering the Nature Reserve of Park Wood and continuing along its bottom edge. At the second notice board, leave the wood along a path into a field and continue in the same direction, crossing a small stream and going below a ruined kiln. Go along a limestone shelf to the left of Cockshott Hill at the top end of a meadow. Join a rough lane leading through the farmyard of Crag House on to the road and turn right, along it to return to Plain Quarry car park.

POINTS OF INTEREST:

There are several springs below Park Wood because here the limestone rests on impervious gritstone.

The descent from the Rakes down Blasterfoot Gap is famed for the rounded, water-eroded channels – karren grooves – which have transformed the area into one of fascinating, beautiful sculpturings.

Walk 50   SALTERFORTH AND DAUBERS   4$\frac{1}{2}$m (7km)

Maps: OS Landranger 103; Pathfinder 670.

A dry weather walk, with a pleasant mixture of walking.

Start: The junction of Salterforth Lane and the B6383.

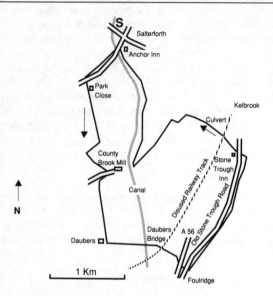

Go along Salterforth Lane, past a footpath sign to 'County Brook', and to the right of Park Close Cottage to cross a stile over the wall ahead. Walk with the wall on your left and go through a gate. Go left to another gate. Follow the cobbled road beyond to Booth House Farm. Go along its boundary wall and bear right to descend a field to a stile in a facing wall. Cross, go between two mounds of earth and over the pasture to a wicket. Continue, crossing a farm track and leaving the field over a stile. The path follows a wall across the next field, leaving over a footbridge. Turn left along a brook to reach a surfaced lane on the right. Go along the lane to a stile in the fence on the left. Cross and follow a path over a meadow, bearing right over a stile. Cross the next field to a stile and continue to a stone stile on the right. Cross and follow a path, leaving the field over a stile on to a track above Hey Fold. Cross it to a stile seen at the end of a fence ahead, beside some hawthorns. Cross a field to a stile before reaching

100

a field gate and a stile ahead. Go along the top of the next field to cross a footbridge in its top right corner. Go between holly trees, crossing the next field to a stile near trees. The path now crosses two stiled fields to reach a grass track. Cross this and go over a stile in the opposite wall. Bear right in the next field, away from a boggy path. Return to your original course and pass the back of Daubers Farm. Turn left, along a track, downhill, to Daubers Bridge over the Leeds and Liverpool Canal. Continue until the track makes a broad left turn. When halfway round this, cross a footbridge near a fence. Go over a stile, across the large pasture ahead and cross a stile on to a lane. Go up a rise to a gate and stile, and walk on to the embankment of the old Skipton-Colne railway. Cross the track bed and go up the field on the top of the embankment. Cross a stile to a path beside the A56. Cross the road to a footpath sign. Go over a stile near a gate and up the road beyond towards a wooded lane and a gate. Beyond this the road leads to Old Stone Trough Lane. Turn left to a road junction at the bottom of Oxenards Avenue. Go along the lane, passing The Old Stone Trough, a large country house. Just beyond it, cross a stile on the left into a field. Go along a path between trees, and bear right to a surfaced road. Go down the pasture to cross a stile in the bottom wall on to a grass verge of the A56. Cross the road to the Stone Trough Inn. Just past it turn right, over a stile near a gate, into a field. Cross this, crossing a stream, then a stile near a culvert. Go under the culvert, turn left, and go through a gate in the field corner. Turn right along a stream almost where the fence on the opposite bank finishes. Now follow a clear path that sweeps round to the left of an earlier path, and continues along a second stream on the right. Go past a wall, cross a stream over a bridge at the top of the pasture and cross a stile in the far fence. Cross the next field on a faint path that keeps to a deep drainage channel on your right. Eventually a footbridge over a stream is seen near a fence ahead: cross it and go straight over a field to reach another footbridge over a deep channel. Go directly ahead to a stile in a fence. Follow the path, first over open pasture, then close to some tall trees on the right, to reach a stile that leads to Mill Bridge, No. 149. Do not cross this bridge. Instead, turn right to a white gate and follow the towpath to Salterforth.

POINTS OF INTEREST:

The low lying, often waterlogged area between the culvert and bridge No. 149, was used as an ammunition dump during the First World War. The titled concrete pedestals were used for raising ammunition from the ground.

REFRESHMENTS:

The Stone Trough Inn, Kelbrook.
The Anchor Inn, Salterforth.

Walk 51   **FRECKLETON AND THE NAZE**   4¹/₂m (7km)

Maps: OS Landranger 102; Pathfinder 688.

*This walk above the tidal creek known as Freckleton Pool is of
particular wildlife interest, since it allows good views of some
of the intertidal habitats of the Ribble Estuary.*

Start: At 425292, the car park beside the school in Freckleton.

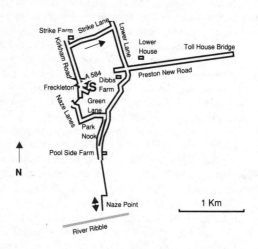

From the car park go to the traffic-lighted junction of Kirkham Road and the A584.
Cross the A584 and continue northwards along Kirkham Road. At Strike Farm turn
right along Strike Lane from where, on a clear day, it is possible to see the imposing
Bleasdale Fells to the north. At the end of Strike Lane, turn right and continue down
Lower Lane until the A584 is reached again. A short detour eastwards along the A584
leads to Halfpenny Hall Bridge where it is still possible to see the remains of the toll
house which remained in operation until the 1920's. The A584, the old marsh road on
which the village of Freckleton lies, linked Preston and Lytham: part of it was a
private turnpike built and operated by Thomas Clifton and Sir Henry Hoghton in the
1780's.

Cross the A584 and go along the lane to Dibb's Farm. At Dibb's Farm take the public footpath to the right of the barn to rejoin Lower Lane. Turn left into Lower Lane and cross it to reach the public footpath signposted 'Warton Brows'. Follow it to Pool Side Farm. Continue past the boatyard, climb the bank and follow the higher path, keeping to the field edges, to reach the triangulation point at the Naze. At this point you are only 46 feet above sea level. The remains of a former shipyard are visible at the Naze: here cargoes were transferred from ocean going ships to smaller 'lighters' that brought the cargo up Dow Brook to Freckleton. Return along the high level path to Park Book through what is an important wildlife habitat, particularly for waders, that forms part of the Ribble Estuary Site of Special Scientific Interest. Frequent visitors here are snipe, lapwing, golden plover, black-tailed godwit, dunlin and greenshank. The pathside meadows contain attractive displays of mayflower and the grassbanks that slope down to the brook abound with common centaury and hawthorn bushes. At Park Nook turn left on to the track which leads to Green Lane, and turn right into Naze Lane. Pass the shops and turn right into the Memorial Playing Fields to return to the centre of **Freckleton**.

POINTS OF INTEREST:

Freckleton – The Ship Inn, in Bunker Street, just off the route, has records that date back to 1770 and is reputed to be much older. It is thought to be the former haunt of smugglers. The Memorial Playing Fields commemorate one of the darkest days in Freckleton's history, an aircraft disaster in 1944 in which many local children lost their lives.

REFRESHMENTS:

There are several pubs in Freckleton, many of which supply bar snacks.

Walk 52   **NEWTON AND SLAIDBURN** $4^1/_2$m (7km)
Maps: OS Sheets Landranger 103; Pathfinder 660.
Outwards over pleasant pastures, returning along the Hodder.
Start: At 696504, the village hall, Newton-In-Bowland.

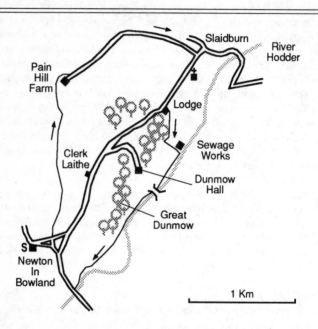

From the hall turn right, through the village, and, where the road forks, keep left, along the main way. Soon, almost opposite a road junction on the right, turn left, as signed, to Pain Hill Moor. Go to the right of a house, then bear right along a path to reach a gate. Continue along a green track, close to the hedge on the right. Go through a gateway close to a stream on the right and, maintain direction across a field. Go through a gap between hawthorns and keep ahead, staying parallel to the stream on the right, to reach a gate. Go through and diagonally left across the field beyond to go through a gate in the top left-hand corner. Continue beside a wall on the left and where it ends, short of a mature copse, cross a stile and walk towards the right-hand side of the copse. On reaching a fence in front of a facing wall, turn left, go over a stile and walk along a green track running parallel to the copse on your left. Beyond the copse, curve right, aiming for the left-hand corner of a facing wall. Cross a ladder stile over the wall on your left and turn right, staying close to the wall on the right, but soon bearing left to go through a gate in a wall. Follow a farm track towards Pain Hill Farm. Go right with it, but before reaching the gate into the farmyard, turn left over a stile. Go forward close to the buildings on the right, and just beyond them turn right, through a gate, on to a farm road. Turn left, along it, for about $1/_2$ mile to reach a gate on to a road. Turn right, descending steeply into Slaidburn.

After passing the Hark to Bounty Inn, on the left, turn right at a road junction and follow the road through Slaidburn, passing the church on the left. Where the road curves right before climbing a hill, go left, as waymarked, through a wicket to the left of the lodge gates. Go along a track to a gate into a field. Go through a kissing gate to the side of a metal one. Go forward into the field for a few yards, then turn left, as directed, to the riverside. Do not cross the stile on the left, just short of the facing gate: instead, continue downstream to reach a bridge over the Hodder. Do not cross: instead, continue along the **riverbank** to go through a kissing gate. Follow the clear path beyond along the foot of a very steep wooded bank. At the end of the wood, go through the left-hand of two wickets and up the field beyond, easing away from the river and aiming for a gateway in its right-hand corner. Short of the gateway, turn right over a stile, cross a ditch and turn left, beside the wall on your left. At a step in the wall go through a gate and cross a bridge over a feeder. Continue along the riverside path to reach a wicket. Cross the field beyond to another wicket on to a road. Turn right back into Newton.

POINTS OF INTEREST:
Riverbank – Much of the Hodder's soft riverbanks between Slaidburn and Newton have been colonised by sand martins. They are migrants, arriving usually in late March or early April and staying until late September or early October, when they fly off to Africa for the winter.

REFRESHMENTS:
The Parkers Arms, Newton-In-Bowland.
The Hark to Bounty Inn, Slaidburn.

Walk 53   CONDER GREEN AND OLD GLASSON   4¹/₂m (7km)

Maps: OS Sheets Landranger 102; Pathfinder 659.

Easy walking throughout.

Start: At 459559, Conder Green car park.

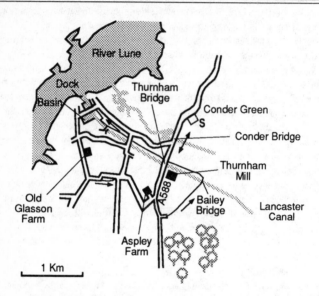

From the **car park** near the Stork Inn at Conder Green go left, southwards, along the A588, with care, until a bridge over the Lancaster Canal is reached. Just short of it, turn left, over a stile, and descend to the canal towpath. Turn right to go under the bridge, No. 6, and walk with the canal on your left. Go under bridges Nos. 7 and 8, then follow the signs for **Glasson Dock** and Basin, passing a parking area and toilets on the right. Turn left between Glasson Basin, on the left, and the Dock, on the right. Now go straight ahead, through the dockyard area and turn left along Tithe Barn Hill. Go ahead at a cross-roads, following Dobs Lane past Old Glasson Farm, on the left, easily identified by its two tall silos.

Where the lane ends, turn left along a cart track. At its end go half-left over a field to reach a gate on to a road. Turn left. The road goes right, then, soon after, left. Here, go ahead along a track which soon bears right to cross four fields before turning left to pass the entrance to Aspley Farm, on the left. Go through a gate and follow a track to the A588. Turn right, with care. Go past a cottage, on the right, and soon after turn left along a track just short of a house on the left. Where the track ends, go straight ahead across a field, aiming for Bailey Bridge, which spans the Lancaster Canal. Cross the bridge and turn right, through a gate, on to the canal towpath. Turn right, go under the bridge and follow the towpath pass a lock with a tall wooden bridge and a weir. Go past Thurnham Mill, once a water-powered cornmill, but now a hotel and restaurant, and another lock. From bridge No. 6, retrace your steps back to the start.

POINTS OF INTEREST:

Car Park – There are two level crossings posts at the entrance to Conder Green car park. They are a reminder that the Lancaster-Glasson Dock Railway once passed through Conder Green.

Glasson Dock – The River Lune had too many shoals and too little deep water, and as the size of ships increased Lancaster declined as a seaport. Glasson was therefore developed, work on the dock starting in 1783. This only partly solved Lancaster's problem, as the town was also too far away from the coal fields and the main manufacturing areas, and its communications inland were poor. It was hoped that the digging of the Lancaster Canal would be a benefit, but the canal cost too much and was too long in the building. It was not completed until 1812, too late to stem the decline in Lancaster's trade. Today Glasson Dock is still operative, but the vessels using it are small coasters and pleasure craft.

REFRESHMENTS:

The Stork Inn, Conder Green.

Thornham Mill, east of Bridge No. 6 on the Lancaster Canal.

Walk 54 FLUKE HALL, BOURBLES, TONGUES LANE 4¹/₂m (7km)

Maps: OS Sheets Landranger 102; Pathfinder 658.

A fine mix of field and coast walking with excellent views across Morecombe Bay.

Start: At 389500, the car parking area near Fluke Hall.

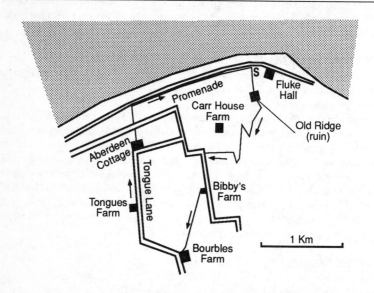

From the car parking area near **Fluke Hall**, cross the road at a Lancaster Port Health Notice and continue southwards, going through a gate into a field. Go across the middle of the field to reach a gate. Go through and maintain direction, between two gate posts, crossing a field close to its right-hand boundary, heading towards ruinous Old Ridge Farm. Go through a gate to the left of the first ruin and walk past ponds on the left, going half-right to reach a gate. Cross the field beyond staying roughly parallel to the right-hand boundary. Go past two trees in rough ground and maintain direction to cross a footbridge over a fenced dyke. Turn right, beside the dyke to reach the right-hand corner of the field. Turn left, edging the field to reach a gate near its right-hand corner. Follow a track close to a hedge on the left across the field beyond to reach a stile in the hedge, close to the corner. Do not cross: instead, turn right and cross the field, edging towards its left-hand boundary and walking along it to go over a stile in the field's left-hand corner.

Continue edging the field beyond, then cross a footbridge and go through a gate on the right. Continue along a farm track on the left to reach a surfaced road. Turn left, along it, to reach Bibby's Farm. Turn right, through the farmyard, going between outbuildings and exiting through a gate. Stay close to the fence on your left to go through another gate. Now go half-right, crossing a concrete road and a bridge over a dyke to the left of a gate. Continue beside a fence and the dyke, leaving the field through a gate in the left-hand corner. Now stay close to the fence on your left to go over a stile in the field corner. Cross an area of rough ground close to the fence on the left and go over a stile on to a track that goes in front of Bourbles Farm. Go along the track, going through a gate to reach a fork. Take the right branch (Tongue Lane). Stay on this lane which, close to Tongue Farm on the left, goes through three gates with adjacent stiles.

On reaching Aberdeen Cottage, where the lane turns sharp right, go straight ahead, beside a dyke on the left, going between buildings on a path that soon crosses a footbridge. Stay beside the dyke, still on your left, to reach a stile. Go over and walk beside a fence on the left. Go through a gate and, a little further on, cross a stile beside a gate to reach a road. Cross and go over the stile opposite. Continue beside a dyke on the right, crossing three stiles to reach an embankment. Turn right, along it, with the southernmost part of **Morecombe Bay** to your left, to return to the car park.

POINTS OF INTEREST:

Fluke Hall – Fluke is a local name for a flatfish. Fluke Hall, now a retirement home, has five fish carved in stone above its entrance.

Morecombe Bay – Together with the Lune estuary, the Bay has one of the largest overwintering and passage populations of wading birds in Britain. It is part of a network of estuaries that form a link between the Arctic and Africa. Regularly there are vast numbers of pink-footed geese, shellduck, pintails, oystercatchers, ringed and grey plovers, knot, dunlin, and turnstones in the Bay. The winter flocks can exceed 200,000 waders and 30,000 wildfowl. At high tide the birds often roost very close to the shore. Good vantage points are Knott End promenade, Fluke Hall and Pilling Lane Ends.

REFRESHMENTS:

Sorry! There are none on this walk, so please bring your own.

Walks 55 & 56   DEERPLAY TO RISING BRIDGE   5m (8km)
or $8^1/_2$m ($13^1/_2$km)

Maps: OS Landranger 103; Pathfinder 689 and 690.
A fine walk around Rossendale Forest.
Start: At 866265, the Deerplay Inn.
Finish: Loveclough, or Rising Bridge.

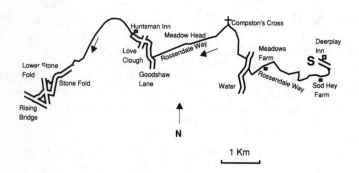

This walk follows a section of the Rossendale Way (marked RW), which can be completed in full by following Walks 55/56, 57/58, 80, 86 and 90/91.

From the **Deerplay Inn**, cross the road and go left into Bacup Old Road. Soon turn right into Harrow Stiles Lane to join the Rossendale Way. Continue to Harrow Hill Farm, leaving it along a green track. Cross a meadow, aiming for the right corner of a building. Turn right, along a track to a ruin, turn left and continue diagonally left over a large field. Turn left, briefly, then right, along a wall. Cross a stile and continue to the right of a waterworks wall. Keep ahead, close to a wall on the left, and where it kinks continue along the waterwork's building wall. Cross a stile, then a field on the left, to reach Meadows Farm. Pass to the right of farm buildings and cross a field towards a pylon. Follow a wall around Lower Clough Bottom and turn right on to Burnley Road East. Go right, to the second track on the left, and go along it for 400 yards. Turn right at a crossing of tracks, going along a grassy path and crossing a catchment channel. Stay on the path for $^1/_2$ mile to reach **Compton's Cross**. Turn left, onto a green track. At Meadow Head take the more obvious track, crossing moorland, and then follow a green path leading to a path in a ravine. Continue through a plantation and turn right into Goodshaw Lane. Go along it, then left at Swinshaw Hall. Descend steps to the A56 at **Loveclough**, the end of a 5 mile long section.

From Loveclough there is a frequent bus service connecting Greater Manchester, Rawtenstall and Burnley. Continue along Commercial Street into a Print Works yard. Follow a clear track and turn left, then right by metal cylinders. When adjacent to the top of a reservoir, leave the track along a fainter one going around the northern end of the Height Cross moorland near a ruinous wall on the left, to turn left on to a track running along the ridge. Soon the track begins to descend: when it bifurcates, go right, towards Lane Top Farm, keeping to the right of a ravine. Where a wall crosses the path, turn right along a wall. Turn right into a farm road from Lane Top Farm and left at a T-junction. Go right into Goodshaw Lane to reach Stone Fold and on to join King's Highway. Turn right in the middle of the village to Lower Stone Fold hamlet the entrance to which is marked by a tree on either side of the road. Just beyond the left tree cross a facing field, aiming for Pewit Hall. Near a stile in the bottom field corner, turn left along a stream. Some 30 yards before a bypass, turn left for 50 yards, then right to reach the Northfield Road. Where this curves left, climb steps to the Blackburn Road at Rising Bridge, having completed $8^1/_2$ miles of walking from the Deerplay Inn.

POINTS OF INTEREST:
The Deerplay Inn – At 1320 feet above sea level, the inn is one of the six highest in England. It was originally on the opposite side of the road, but moved to the present building, formerly a farmhouse, about the middle of the 19th century.
Compton's Cross – Erected by Samuel Compton, a local historian and ex-Mayor of Rawtenstall, in 1902 at a meeting place of trackways.
Loveclough – The name means a clough near lying water.

REFRESHMENTS:
The Deerplay Inn.
The Huntsman Inn, Loveclough.
The Rising Bridge Inn, Rising Bridge.

Walks 57 & 58   RISING BRIDGE TO CLOUGH HEAD   5m (8km)

or 13$\frac{1}{2}$m (21$\frac{1}{2}$km)

Maps: OS Landranger 103; Pathfinder 689 and 700.

A fine walk around Rossendale Forest.

Start: At 782256, the Rising Bridge Inn.

Finish: Clough Head Quarry or the Irwell Bridge.

This walk follows a section of the Rossendale Way (marked RW), which can be completed in full by following Walks 55/56, 57/58, 80, 86 and 90/91.

From the Inn turn left into Roundhill Lane. Cross a railway bridge and bear left to reach Roundhill Road near the Farmer's Glory. Continue along Moor Lane, past Moor Lane Farm. At the lane end, walk with the wall on the left, then over open moor towards Copy Farm seen on the horizon. Pass the farm close to a wall on the left. Cross a field and turn sharp right along a clear track. At Windy Harbour Farm take a waymarked field track to Picker Hill and continue along another track. Ignoring a steeply climbing grassy track on your right, go towards some isolated trees. Just beyond these go left along a rough track to reach three trees beyond some ruins. The way is now less well-defined: a track skirts Heap Clough Quarry Workings and climbs to ruinous Dilly Moor. Beyond, two fields are crossed to reach another ruin. A group of trees marks another ruin, and another is soon reached. Continue behind a woodland area to reach a stile in the fence to the left. Cross the stile and a meadow to reach Grove Road. Turn left to Clough Head Quarry Car Park, the end of a 5 mile walk.

There is an infrequent bus service along the Haslingden Grove road, beside the quarry, linking Blackburn, Haslingden, Rawtenstall and Rochdale.

From the car park, go right for $^1/_2$ mile, then go left following an 'Egerton Moss' signpost. After 300 yards go left along a sunken track, passing ruinous Close Bottom and Peak, to join a track. Continue to Top-of-th'-Knoll, bridge a stream, edge a wood and a small quarry, and go on to reach Grane Head. Turn left, then right, on to the Calf Hey Trail. At point 8 on this trail go ESE towards Clough side. Turn left and walk past conifers for $^1/_2$ mile. Pass a barn, cross a stream and fork right uphill towards a ruinous chimney. Follow an old tramway for 200 yards, and take a sunken track for 20 yards. Fork right for 100 yards, then left for 150 yards. Continue to Rushy Leach ruins. Pass Bailiff's Rake, then go right, along a green track, to Musden Head. Cross two streams, ford Long Grain Water and look back along the valley side. The path now climbs steeply and crosses a large field on a clear track to reach a concrete road leading to the Great House Farm complex. Turn right at an access gate and follow a farm track past three former farms. Below the site of Spring Bank Farm, bear left and continue over the moor to Alden Brook. Go past ruinous Goose Pits, round the shoulder of Bull Hill and follow a faint trod across open moor. Descend into a shallow ravine. Cross the 'moor road' and Helmshore Road, and follow the track opposite. Soon turn right to reach Higher Buckden Farm. Cross a field and enter **Buckden Woods**. Cross a footbridge and go left along a path that becomes progressively clearer. Ignore a footbridge to 'The Cliffe' and keep ahead to reach a surfaced road. Turn left, go under two railway bridges, and on to an unsurfaced riverside track for 200 yards. Go right, into Chatterton village to reach Bolton Road adjacent to the bridge over the Irwell where the walk ends.

POINTS OF INTEREST:
Buckden Woods – Col Stubbins, who died a millionaire, left 435 acres and 8 farms to the National Trust in 1943. The bequest included Buckden Woods.

REFRESHMENTS:
The Rising Bridge Inn, Rising Bridge.
The Farmer's Glory, Rising Bridge.
The Duke of Wellington (along Grove Road).

Walk 59   **ARNSIDE AND ARNSIDE KNOTT**   5m (8km)

Maps: OS Landranger 97; Pathfinder 636.

The best walk in the book, partly along the finest coastal footpath in the North-West.

Start: At 453786, the south end of the promenade, Arnside.

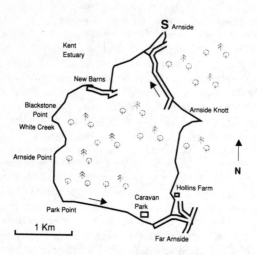

From the south end of the promenade follow a concrete path up some steps into a narrow reserve. Go through to reach some information notice boards at the far end. Continue along the pebbly shoreline, through an area rich in fossils where calcide crystals make the rocks shimmer like diamonds. On reaching a creek, beyond which the cottages of New Barns are seen, resist the temptation to cross it. Instead, follow the shoreline, soon crossing the creek on a bridge. If the tide is in, continue along a cliff top path to the southern end of it at Blackstone Point. Otherwise go along the foot of the cliffs, on the sand. Continue round the point to lovely, wooded White Creek Bay, edging the pebble beach to a path at its far end. Climb the path to reach a broader one at a footpath sign for 'White Creek – Far Arnside'. Turn right for ¹/₂ mile of glorious cliff top walking past Arnside Point and Park Point. Turn right, through a secluded caravan site and along a tarmac lane to Far Arnside. After 100 yards turn left along a signposted footpath and cross a field to join another track at Hollins Farm, with Arnside Knott clearly seen on the left. The path climbs diagonally right from the farm to enter woods at a junction of paths. Continue across a broad track that curves gently to westwards, and take a slimmer one that climbs past a seat to a level shoulder of land. Beyond this follow a broad path along the crest of the hill to see a knotted tree. This is one of a pair which were knotted in Victorian times as the landmark of Arnside Knott. Sadly, the only remaining one is now dead. Descend a steep path beyond it to cross a stile and go over a field to a road. Turn right and descend into Arnside. At a bend in the road, either follow a footpath sign back to the shore or continue along the road for a further 100 yards before going left, along a footpath, down to the shore close to the south end of Arnside promenade.

POINTS OF INTEREST:
An ornithologist's delight, this enchanting walk is one to savour, but be warned: you could be smitten, overcome with the desire to return to it again and again.

REFRESHMENTS:
Hotels, pubs and cafés in Arnside.

Walk 60   WHITEWELL AND CRIMPTON   5m (8km)

Maps: OS Sheets Landranger 103; Pathfinder 669.

A delightful, airy walk above the valley that cradles the Hodder.

Start: At 659469, Whitewell Village Green.

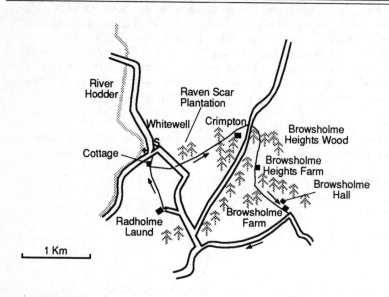

From the green cross the road and continue uphill. Just past a private lane, on the right, climb signed steps, also on the right, to a gate. Cross a field to a track just before a cottage. Cross and continue up the field. Once past the cottage, go half-right and continue uphill close to a line of trees. Go through a gate and continue along a track. Where this forks take the left-hand branch. Go through a gate, cross a road and through a facing gate. Go half-right along a signed track, but where it curves left, go straight ahead to cross the remains of a wall. Continue parallel to a wooded gill, then close to a wall on the right. Where this curves across you, go through a gap, cross a fence and climb a field, aiming for the left corner of a copse. Keep ahead, along the left side of a depression, then aim for a stile in a facing wall. Go over and immediately bear left to cross a stile into a plantation. Follow a path through, then beside, the plantation, with a fence now on your left. Go over a stile and turn right. Now bear slightly left, away from the fence, following waymarkers across a field to a gate. Go through a small wood, exiting through a wicket beside a gate. Go along the fence on your right to reach a farm building, on the right. Go over a waymarked stile and continue to Crimpton Farm. Turn left, as waymarked, between buildings, then go along the farm road to a T-junction. Turn right along a road for a few yards, then go left, over a stile into a plantation. Go half-right up through the plantation, leaving over a stile. Turn left to a fence corner, then bear right, aiming for a building to the left of a wood. Cross a farm road close to the wood, then go over a waymarked stile. Walk along a lane, then bear right to cross a stile in a facing fence, passing Browsholme Heights Farm on the left. Go down a field, pass a building, left, then go half-left, aiming to the left of the furthermost pylon. A facing fence protrudes towards you: aim for the right-hand corner to leave the field over a stile. Turn right, pass a pond, left, and cross a stile. Go ahead, descending towards the left side of a wood. Go over a stile and down a lane to reach another stile. Cross a field ahead, going to the right of a clump of trees to reach a gate on to a track. Turn right towards Browsholme Farm. Go through a gate on to a road. Browsholme Hall and the Farm are to the left, but you turn right to reach a road. Turn right again, and, after $3/4$ mile, turn right at a road junction. Follow the road for $1/2$ mile, then turn left along the road to Radholme Laund Farm. Go through the farmyard, passing in front of the farmhouse, and, at the end of the building on your right, turn right through a gate into a field. Go along the wall on your right to reach a kissing gate. Now go half-right across a field to reach a kissing gate in the wall on the right. Go through, turn left and cross a field to a gate in the left corner of a facing wall. Continue along the wall on the left, descending to where the wall goes left. There, bear right, keeping left of a concrete structure to cross a stile. Keep descending, aiming for the left-hand side of the cottage passed on the outward leg. Cross a track to the cottage and retrace your steps back into Whitewell.

REFRESHMENTS:
The Whitewell Inn, Whitewell.

Walk 61   WEST BRADFORD AND GRINDLETON   5m (8km)

Maps: OS Sheets Landranger 103; Pathfinder 669.

A most enjoyable walk through typical Ribble Valley scenery.

Start: At 743444; the Three Millstones Inn, West Bradford.

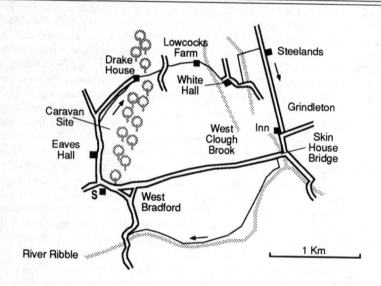

From theInn turn left, along the road to reach a junction. Turn right: the road goes uphill, then levels out, then bends left and climbs again. Between the bend and the road sign ahead, turn right, up a bank, going between gateposts into the left corner of a caravan site. Stay close to the hedge on the left, then turn left over a stile near an oak and bear right to cross a culvert. Turn left into a camping area and go along the woodland edge on the left to reach a road where it curves right. Beyond the bend, keep ahead towards woodland on the left and cross a stile into a paddock. Exit over a stile and cross a second paddock to another stile. Cross a third paddock, bearing left beside a fenced enclosure to reach its end. Turn right, cross a stile and continue to a kissing gate. Go diagonally left, passing outbuildings and Drake House to reach a gate. Go through and along a descending, unsurfaced track through woods to ford a stream. Keep on the track, at first edging a stream on the right, then climbing and curving left. Ignore a ladder stile on the right, staying on the track to the top of the bank. Go over a stile and bear half-right to reach a stile, on the right. Go over and turn left through a facing fence.

Cross the field beyond to a stile on the left of the facing fence. Cross the next field, close to the fence on the left, exiting over a stile in the left-hand corner of a facing fence. Cross a field, keeping to the right of a little wood. Cross a culvert and continue to cross a stile on to a road. Go left, then right at a T-junction to reach Lowcocks Farm. Cross the farmyard, leaving through a gate and follow a curving track. Where this splits, go right, go over a stile and cross a field, staying close to the fence on the right. Enter woodland and descend to cross West Clough Brook. Now go half-right to reach a gate. Continue diagonally right, climb a bank and continue parallel to, and above, a stream on the right. Go over a stile to the right of two hawthorns and cross a field to another stile. Go diagonally left across the next field, exiting over a cattle grid. Go forward, briefly, then left along a farm road. Where this splits, go right along a steeply descending road. After bridging a stream at the foot of the hill, go left over a stile and immediately turn left to cross a stream. Turn right, upstream, go through a gap in a fence and, soon after crossing a tiny feeder, cross the stream on a footbridge. Turn left along the bottom of the hillside, at first following the stream, then moving away from it to leave the field through a gate on to a road. Turn right along this quiet road, soon going through Grindleton. At the southern end of the village turn right along a road that immediately curves left. Soon, turn right and cross Skin House Bridge. Just past a house beyond, turn left along a signed, fenced path to the River Ribble. Turn right along the river crossing a bridge over a feeder. Continue across a field, leaving it by a concrete bridge over another feeder.

Turn left, back to the river and turn right along it. Where the river sweeps left, the path continues straight ahead, keeping to the right of some low ground to cross a stile and then continuing diagonally left to rejoin the river. Continue downstream, crossing a bridge over a feeder. Next, you briefly leave the Ribble to bridge another feeder, returning to the river. Soon after, go over a stile on the right on to the road. Turn right back into West Bradford.

REFRESHMENTS:
The Three Mill Stones, West Bradford.
The Buck Inn, Grindleton.

Walk 62   **NEWTON AND ROUGH SYKE BARN**   5m (8km)
Maps: OS Sheets Landranger 103; Pathfinder 660.
A fine blend of fields and moorland.
Start: At 696504, the village hall, Newton-In-Bowland.

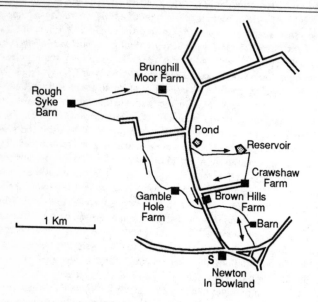

From the village hall turn right, through the village, and where the road forks, keep left. Soon, almost opposite a road junction on the right, turn left along a signed, unsurfaced drive towards a large house. Keep to the left of the house and cross a ladder stile into a field. Bear left and uphill to reach a waymarked stile. Go over and turn right down the field beyond to reach the corner of a wall that comes halfway across the field. Turn right, along the wall, and, short of a farm building, turn left over a stile. Walk across the field beyond, at first on rising ground. Where you start to descend, turn left, along a track that goes diagonally across the field. Cross a stream, climb a bank and bear left to reach a waymarked stile on to a road. Cross diagonally left and turn right through a recessed gate into a field. Cross diagonally left to reach a stile. Go over and cross the next field along a track leading to Gamble Hole Farm. On reaching the farm road, turn left, through a gate into the farmyard, passing buildings on the left. Go through a gate into the field, and halfway across it, bear right and continue down its middle, walking parallel to the wall on your right and keeping to the left of a pond. On reaching a depression, go diagonally left to reach a wicket into a lane, reaching it as it curves right away from you. Continue straight ahead, along the lane, which soon turns sharp left. Do likewise, but leave the lane at a facing gate into rough pasture. Go diagonally right, as directed by a yellow arrow, along a descending track to reach a stile.

Go over and maintain direction, descending along a track. Just short of a building, Rough Syke Barn, leave the track, turning sharp right along a narrow, contouring path. Where the path splits, take the right-hand branch that climbs slightly, passing to the right of an ash tree. Where the path fades, continue contouring towards a wall. There, bear right, uphill slightly, to cross a stile. Cross the field beyond, and on reaching a facing wall turn right along it to reach a stile. Cross to reveal a yellow arrow on its far side confirming your route. Go straight ahead to reach a ladder stile in the facing wall. Go over and straight ahead across a field, leaving it through a gate. Bear right, skirting a copse, and on reaching a facing gate turn right and continue alongside the wall on your left, leaving the field through a gate close to its left-hand corner. Go diagonally left across the next field, exiting through a gate on to a road. Turn right, briefly, to reach a signed path just beyond a fenced pond on the left. Go over a stile and diagonally right across the field beyond to reach a stile over a wall. Go straight across the field beyond, cross a stile and maintain direction to go over a stile. Go diagonally right across the large pasture beyond, aiming for a clump of trees surrounding a reservoir. From there continue towards a facing wall and turn right, along it. Cross a stile in a facing wall and turn right, down a field, leaving through a gate near the bottom right-hand corner. Continue down a lane, passing Crawshaw Farm on the left. Cross a cattle grid and follow the farm road to its end. Turn left, along a road, soon passing Brown Hills Farm on the left. Just beyond, at a footpath sign, the outward leg is rejoined. Turn left here and retrace your steps to Newton.

REFRESHMENTS:
The Parkers Arms, Newton-In-Bowland.

Walk 63   WITHNELL FOLD NATURE RESERVE   5m (8km)

Maps: OS Sheets Landranger 103; Pathfinder 689.
A delightful canal towpath walk to a Nature Reserve.
Start: At 624252, Finnington's Marina.

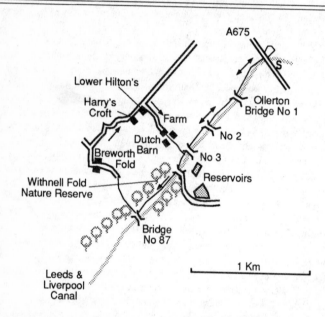

From the entrance to the Marina turn right along the roadside pavement, cross the canal bridge and turn right, through a gate, to reach the towpath of the Leeds and Liverpool canal. Turn right along the towpath, going under the bridge you have just crossed. At the next bridge, Ollerton No. 1, go under, continuing along the towpath. Ahead is the chimney belonging to an old **Wiggins Teape** paper mill. Go under Ollerton No. 2 bridge and continue to Ollerton No. 3. The **Withnell Fold Nature Reserve** is sited close to this bridge. Do not turn left to cross the canal on this bridge: instead, continue straight ahead, through a wicket. Now from the Nature Reserve notice board, go right, down steps, into the Reserve. On leaving the Reserve at this same point turn right, along the towpath, going under a bridge and continuing to the next one, No. 87. Here, bear right away from the towpath and climb a path to a stile at the right-hand side of the bridge. Go over and descend steeply, going diagonally right to the foot of the slope. Turn right, walk to the right-hand corner of a field and cross a stile into a wood. Cross a stream over a footbridge and go straight up the wooded bank ahead on a path to a stile. Go over and cross the field beyond, staying close to a fence on the left. Where it ends, bear slightly left along a depression in the hillside.

As you walk along this, on rising ground, curve right to reach a stile a little to the left of a gate. Go over and continue along a lane to Breworth Fold Farm. Go through the farmyard, between buildings, and turn along a tarmac lane to reach a T-junction. Turn right along a lane. Ignore a footpath sign and stile on the right as the road turns left, staying on the road to pass Harry's Croft, on the right, and Lower Hinton's, also on the right. A little further on, turn right along a lane, as directed by a footpath sign. The lane ends at a farm: continue over the field ahead, passing a Dutch barn, on the right, and another building, on the left, to reach a stile into a field. Keep straight ahead, close to a fence, then a hedge, on your right. Exit over a stile near the field's left-hand corner and descend into woodland. Go diagonally right along a path, and at the bottom of a shallow valley cross a footbridge. Beyond, where the path forks, take the left-hand, uphill, branch. Go over a stile and turn right along a lane. At its end, turn left along the towpath and retrace your steps, most pleasantly, back to the Marina.

POINTS OF INTEREST:

Wiggins Teape – The village of Withnell Fold was purpose-built to house Wiggins Teape paper mill workers. Paper manufactured at the mill was used for printing money at the Royal Mint.

Withnell Fold Nature Reserve – The area was developed as a series of filter beds and sludge gills for the Wiggins Teape paper mill which stood on the eastern side of the canal. Disused and deserted for many years, it has been reclaimed by nature. The lagoons and the filter beds have been in-filled with silt and reed swamp, while further north, the former waste tip has been overgrown with scrub. Today the area is home to a wide variety of plants and animals. The Reserve's splendid bird hide is both a pleasing and a useful feature. Paths link the lagoons, which very well constructed wooden walkways span, thus allowing close observation of the pond life.

REFRESHMENTS:

The Boatyard Inn, Finnington's Marina.

Walk 64   THE LANCASTER CANAL AT BROCK   5m (8km)

Maps: OS Sheets Landranger 102; Pathfinder 668 and 679.

The Lancaster Canal is a pleasant and interesting companion, the surrounding countryside quiet and restful.

Start: At 512406, the road bridge over the River Brock at Brock.

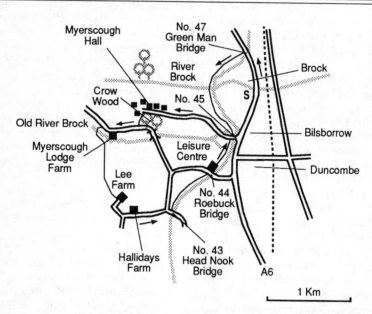

From the bridge, at the northern end of Brock village, go north, with care, along the A6 for about 200 yards to where the road crosses the **Lancaster Canal** on bridge No. 47. Do likewise, then immediately turn right, down steps, to the canal towpath. Turn right to go underneath the bridge and continue along the towpath. For $\frac{1}{2}$ mile the canal heads south-westwards in a straight line before curving left to cross the River Brock on a single span, 60 feet long, aqueduct. Continue along the towpath, soon passing a copse, where the canal curves to the right. Soon after, bridge No. 45 is reached. Go under it and at once climb steps up to a quiet road. Turn left along it to pass, after about $\frac{1}{2}$ mile, Crow Wood, on the left. Beyond this, continue along a track which passes between buildings of the College of Education at Myerscough Hall.

Beyond these buildings the track curves left to reach a road. Turn right, for $\frac{1}{2}$ mile to where, just past Myerscough Lodge Farm, on the left, the road turns sharp right. There, turn left along a footpath. Almost at once cross Old River Brock over a stone footbridge and immediately turn left alongside it.

Where the river curves left, cross a farm track and keep straight ahead, staying close to a hedge on your right. Cross a stile in a fence and keep ahead, crossing Withney Dyke on a stone bridge and continuing close to the hedge on your left. The way now becomes more distinct, developing into a track which is paved in places. Soon it curves left towards Lee Farm. When it leads to a barn, go straight ahead through a gate on to the farm road. Turn right, following the road as it turns left and reaches a Y-junction with Moss Lane. Turn left along the lane, soon passing Hallidays Farm. Where the lane turns sharp left, go right along a tarmac path to reach bridge No. 43 on the Lancaster Canal. Go through a gate on the left and descend steps on to the towpath. Turn left along the towpath. Just beyond bridge No. 44, in the middle of a leisure complex, a thatched building, Owd Nell's Tavern, well worth a visit, is reached. Continue along a towpath, through Bilsborrow, soon reaching bridge No. 45. Climb the steps used on the outward leg and turn right to the junction with the A6. Turn left, with great care, for $\frac{1}{4}$ mile to reach the bridge over the River Brock where this gentle walk began.

POINTS OF INTEREST:

Lancaster Canal – Snaking through a gentle landscape richly carpeted with great drifts of wild flowers in season, the Lancaster Canal at Brock attracts a great many people, boat dwellers, walkers and those simply seeking a place in which to relax. It is that sort of environment: yet it is not without an interesting history. There are some old milestones along this stretch of the canal which give the distances from Preston to Garstang. By referring to them, bargees could decide when to rest their horses. Brock aqueduct, No. 46, which has a 60 foot single span, carries the canal over the River Brock at a height of some 22 feet. It was designed by John Rennie who, that same year (1797) built the canal aqueduct over the Lune to a design by Alexander Stevens.

REFRESHMENTS:

Owd Nell's Tavern, Roebuck Bridge (No. 44).
The Roebuck, Bilsborrow.
There are also possibilities at the Leisure Complex.

Walk 65   MARLES WOOD AND COPSTER GREEN   5m (8km)

Maps: OS Sheets Landranger 103; Pathfinder 680.

A pleasant mixture of riverside walking, woodland and fields.

Start: At 675355, the car park at Marles Wood.

From the car park go northwards along a footpath through Marles Wood and, on reaching the River Ribble, turn right along a track that follows the riverbank upstream, going through Marles Wood at first, then across fields. After $\frac{3}{4}$ mile a footbridge, **Dinckley Bridge**, is reached. Do not cross: instead, continue upstream to join the road to **Dinckley Hall**. On reaching the Hall, turn right, and soon leave the road through a waymarked gate on the left. Go diagonally left to reach a tree waymarked with a white footpath sign. Turn right and walk to a stile at the end of the field. Go over and turn right, staying close to the hedge on the right to reach a stile. Go over to reach Cravens Farm. Continue straight ahead along the farm track to a road and turn left along it. As you approach Aspinall's Farm, turn right, over a stile, and go straight across the field beyond to reach another stile. Go over and maintain direction to reach a gate. Go through and walk ahead to go through a gap in the facing hedge. Maintain direction to reach Wardfall Farm. Go along the farm road to reach a road. Cross, go over a stile into a field and go diagonally right across it, exit at its top right-hand corner.

Go past a humpback bridge, on your left, that spans Dinckley Brook and, a little further on, enter the field ahead. Immediately turn right and go diagonally left across it. The field is long and narrow: leave it close to its left-hand corner to reach a tarmac track. Turn left, along the track to Dinckley Grange, which you pass on your left. Just beyond it, bear right, soon reaching a waymarked tree. Continue to reach a waymarked stile. Go over and keep ahead to reach a drystone stile. Go over and cross the next field, aiming for a footbridge over Park Brook. Cross and head for a sheep pen ahead, continuing along a track to reach a road. Turn right, briefly, then go right again, into Park Gate Row. Follow the track between houses, passing Bolton Hall on the left, and continue through the farmyard to reach a gate. Go through and turn right, crossing the field beyond close to its right-hand side, and leaving close to its right-hand corner, as signposted.

Go diagonally left across the next field to reach its left-hand corner, then diagonally right across the next field to reach Marles Wood. As you cross this last field, Park Wood is seen edging it on the left. This part of the walk from Park Gate has been well signposted, with tall white posts marking the route. Continue northwards, through **Marles Wood**, to reach the Ribchester road. Turn right to return to the car park.

POINTS OF INTEREST:

Dinckley Bridge and Hall – The word Dinckley is Celtic. Dinckley Bridge crosses the River Ribble at a point where for many centuries before its construction people were ferried across it. The Talbot family, local minor gentry, built Dinckley Hall in the 16th century and it is said that it was a hiding place for Royalists during the Civil War. The hall, which has a medieval cruck frame, is a listed building.

Marles Wood – At one time the whole of the Ribble Valley hereabouts was forested. Marles Wood is a remnant of that forest. It is home to a rich variety of wildlife including herons and hares. Flag iris and many other species of flower can also be found there.

REFRESHMENTS:
The Park Gate Inn, Copster Green.
The Tanners Arms, Ribchester Road, Dinckley.
The Blackbull Hotel, Old Langho.

Walk 66   **OVERTON AND SUNDERLAND POINT**   5m (8km)
Maps: OS Sheets Landranger 102; Pathfinder 659.
An easy walk with splendid views across Morecambe Bay.
Start: At 434579, the car park opposite the Globe Hotel, Overton.

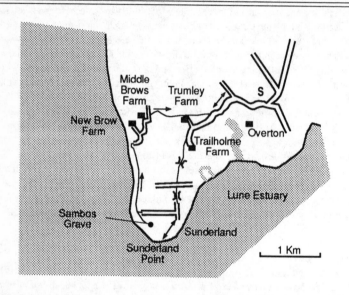

From the car park turn right along a hedged lane, marked as a cul-de-sac, leading to
Trailholme Farm. Skirt the northern edge of Lades Marsh staying on the main lane to
pass the entrance to Trumley Farm. Continue along the lane towards Trailholme Farm,
but before reaching it, where the lane turns half-left before heading straight towards
the farm, cross a stile on the right on to a track. Turn left, along it, passing Trailhome
Farm, on the left. Continue along a concrete flagged causeway. Go over a stile and
turn right, staying on the stiled causeway that runs along the top of a low embankment.
Turn left into a field, crossing to a step stile. Go over and diagonally left to cross a
footbridge in the left-hand corner of the field. Keep ahead, beside a hedge and then a
stream to cross a farm track near another footbridge. Stay on the same side of the
stream to reach another bridge in the field corner. Cross and follow a grassy track that
curves left, then right, to go along an embankment. Go over a stile at the foot of the

embankment, climb steps and go over another stile. Go right, along the embankment, to join the tidal road (so called because at every high tide it is under water) to Sunderland. Go in front of some cottages, along a lane, passing the old harbour area. Continue along the foreshore, passing the end of a terrace to reach the Old Hall. Progress to Sunderland Point entails a scramble over stones and breakwaters, but the foreshore is fascinating and well worth a visit.

There is no path round the headland, so retrace your steps to the end of Second Terrace. Now turn left, away from the shore, along a bridlepath (The Lane) signed for West Shore, following it to the western foreshore. Here a short detour of 150 yards is recommended: turn left and, just past a bench, go over a signed stile into a field to reach the grave of **Sambo**. Retrace your steps to where The Lane meets the foreshore and continue northwards past an area of marsh. From the bridleway Heysham nuclear power station is seen ahead. On reaching the bungalow at Potts Corner the bridleway joins a lane from the caravan site at Middleton Sands. Go along this, passing Hawthorne House Farm, right, and New and Middle Brows Farms, left. The lane now turns sharp right, then sharp left. Just beyond this latter corner, turn right, along a signed path to Middleton. Walk beside a stream, then go over a stile and continue to reach a stile in the fence on the right. Go over and aim for a stile to the left of Trumley Farm. Go over on to a path behind the farm, following it across a field to reach the lane used on the outward leg. Turn left to retrace your steps back to the start.

POINTS OF INTEREST:

Sambo – A little West Indian boy servant of a sea captain, Sambo, died of a fever, following a voyage from the West Indies. His death occurred in 1735 in the loft of Upstairs Cottage, Sunderland. The building is so named because its steps are on its outside. Because Sambo was a slave, he was not allowed to be buried in consecrated ground and was laid to rest in a field overlooking Morecambe Bay. In later years, as opposition to slavery and the slave trade grew, Sambo became a symbol of that exploitation.

REFRESHMENTS:
The Globe Hotel, Overton.

Walk 67 LONGTON AND WALMER BRIDGE 5m (8km)

Maps: OS Sheets Landranger 102; Pathfinder 688.

A walk specially designed for both able bodied people and those in wheelchairs.

Start: At 479251, a car park on the main road into Longton.

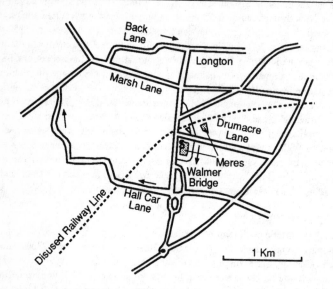

This walk is rather special as it has been designed for use by people in wheelchairs. All the stiles are negotiable by wheelchairs and much of the walking surfaces is excellent.

There is a toilet for the disabled at the public convenience opposite the Rams Head, Longton, but a key for it has to be purchased from the Environmental Health and Housing Department, Civic Centre, West Paddock, Leyland. However, the library and the health centre, both nearby, have toilets for the disabled.

The car park lies just south of the junction with Drumacre Lane, and is close to some meres that used to be old brick pits. From it turn right, southwards, along a path that edges a mere and continue straight ahead to go over a stile on to a road close to its junction with the main road, on the right. Cross this road and keep straight ahead, going alongside the main road to reach a cross-roads after about $1/2$ mile. Turn right, along Hall Carr Lane, using the footpath as far as a sign on the left to 'Hoole'. Continue westwards along the lane, soon passing under a now demolished bridge that once carried the Preston to Southport railway line. Continue along the lane which turns right, then left, then curves more gently to the right and goes past a junction, on the right, with Hall Lane.

Continue to the end of Hall Carr Lane, then turn right along Marsh Lane. Go past a turning on the left, then, soon after Marsh Lane makes a fairly sharp turn right, take the next turning to the left (Back Lane). Soon, Back Lane loses its good surface and becomes grassy: continue along it until just before a built up area (**Longton**) is reached. Now turn right, along a footpath that goes southwards, leading back to Marsh Lane which it reaches at its junction with the main road. Cross, with care, and walk southwards along it, in the direction of Walmer Bridge. Just beyond Woodlands Way, turn left through some metal gates and follow a path diagonally right through a pleasant, lightly wooded area, along which seats have been provided by a thoughtful council. The path leads to School Lane: turn left along it, passing Ashwood Court on the right and entering Briarcroft. Immediately turn right, along a path that leads over a stile to the meres. Continue with the northernmost mere on your left, then walk past another, on the right, to reach Drumacre Lane. Cross and follow an elevated path that curves right, edging the largest mere to return to the car park.

POINTS OF INTEREST:

Longton – Longton is an old village, strongly associated with the brick making industry. When the brickworks closed, the brick pits filled with water and, with a little help from the local authority, the area was allowed to revert to nature. Shrubs, trees and water-loving flora were encouraged, the harsh scars of industry mellowed and the result is a most pleasing environment. A rich variety of water fowl can now be found on the meres, including mallard, tufted duck, greylag and pink footed geese, coots, moorhens, grebes and swans. Longton itself has grown considerably, and is now a dormitory suburb of Preston.

REFRESHMENTS:

The Golden Ball Inn, Longton.
The Longton Tavern, Longton.
The Rams Head Inn, Longton.
The Anchor Hotel, Longton.
The Forshaws Café, Longton.

Walk 68   HORNBY AND GRESSINGHAM   5m (8km)

Maps: OS Sheets Landranger 97; Pathfinder 637.

A nice blend of riverside, field, lane and quiet road walking.

Start: At 585685, St Margaret's Church, Hornby.

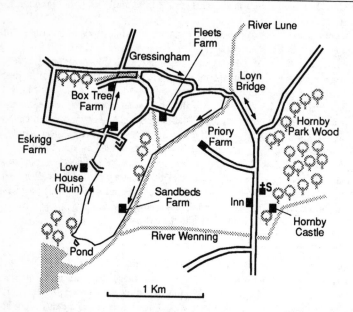

From the church, turn right, through Hornby and at a junction at the north end of the village, go diagonally left along the road for Gressingham. Cross the River Lune on Loyn Bridge, then turn left over a waymarked stile and go down to the riverside. Cross a fence and walk downstream. At the end of the field, turn right to reach a waymarked footbridge into woodland. Continue along a path that soon returns to the riverbank. Now stay with the river, crossing several stiles to reach the confluence of the rivers Wenning and Lune. Continue downstream to where the Lune makes a slight turn left. There, walk ahead, aiming for a hut and crossing a stile in front of it. Turn right and aim for the right-hand corner of a pond, just in front of Crow Wood. Pass the pond, then bear left up a track to a gate into Crow Wood. Go through and turn right, along a track. Where the track curves left into private property, walk ahead along an unsurfaced track which also curves left. On the bend, go through a gate on the right into a field and cross half-left to a gate. Cross the field beyond, going half-right, aiming for the right-hand side of a row of trees that crosses the hill's brow. Go through a gate and continue along the hedge on the left. A track develops: continue along until you are on level ground, then go half-left through a gate at a step in the hedge. Maintain direction, with a hedge/fence on the right to reach the field corner. Turn left along the line of an old lane and at the bottom, turn half-right along another old lane, going to the right of a ruin (Low House). On reaching a gate on the right, go through and half-left across the corner of a field to reach a stile.

Go over and cross the field beyond, passing a building to the left. Go through gate in the corner and cross the next field, passing some renovated properties on the left. Go over a stile and turn right, along a lane to a cross-roads. Go straight over, on a lane signed for Eskrigg House. Passing the house, on the right, and keep ahead through a waymarked gate. Cross the field beyond to reach a waymarked stile. Go straight ahead, descending steeply to reach a waymarked stile to the left of a gate beneath an oak. Cross a field beside a fence on the left to reach a waymarked stile. Go over and cross a narrow field to join a farm track. Follow this to reach a road. Turn left towards Box Tree Farm, on the right. Just short of it, turn right down a lane to a footbridge over a stream. Cross a second footbridge and continue along the lane to reach the road through Gressington. Turn right and follow the road to Loyn Bridge. Now retrace your steps back to the church.

REFRESHMENTS:
The Castle Hotel, Hornby.

Walks 69 & 70   **GARSTANG**   5m (8km)
                                              or 6m (9$\frac{1}{2}$km)

Maps: OS Sheets Landranger 102; Pathfinder 668.
A field walk with good views of the coast and the Irish Sea.
Start: At 493454, the Community Centre car park, Garstang.

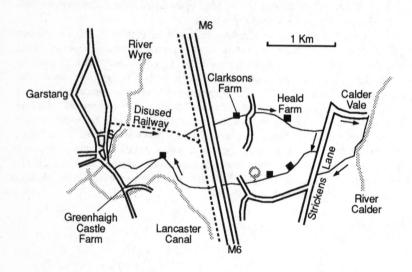

Walk upstream, along the Wyre's riverbank to reach a bridge. Climb steps to reach an old railway track bed. Turn right, over the bridge and follow the track over four stiles to reach a cutting. Do not enter: instead, climb the bank on the left, cross a stile and go half-right across a field to reach a ladder stile. Follow a track over a railway line and the M6, continuing along a lane, passing Clarkson's Farm, on the left. Cross a road at a double bend, going along a concrete road and then following a track beside Heald Wood, on the left, towards Heald Farm. Just short of the farmhouse go left, over a stile into a wood. Cross rough ground close to a stile. Go left through a gate near a barn, and turn right beside the hedge on the right to reach a stile. Cross this and two further stiles to reach Strickens Lane.

The shorter route turns right here, following the lane to reach a cottage, Walker

House, on the left, where the longer route is rejoined.

The longer route crosses the lane and goes through the middle of three gates beside a bungalow. Walk beside a fence on the right, cross a waymarked stile and cross a field to another a stile. Turn left over a footbridge and cross the field beyond to a stile. Now follow a path beside a wood, then go behind houses and descend steps to a road in Calder Vale village. Cross and turn right, briefly, then bear left along Albert Terrace. Continue along a track beside the River Calder, on the left, soon passing a mill lodge. Cross the river, go past cottages and a barrier, and where the track splits, go right, climbing out of the woods to go through a gate into a field. Cross to another gate and continue along a lane, passing Sullom Side Farm, on the right, to reach Strickens Lane. Turn right to reach Walker House and the shorter route.

Go over a stile beside a gate and cross a field to a gate in the right-hand corner. Go half-left across the next field to enter Lucas's Farmyard. Cross and turn left along a lane in front of the farmhouse. After 20 yards turn right through a gate. Edge a field to a stile and cross the next field aiming to the right of the buildings of Lower House Farm. Go through a gate and turn right through another. Go along a lane into a field and cross it to a stile in the bottom left-hand corner. Walk along the left edge of next field to a stile. Walk beside a wood on the right, cross a stile and another stile on your right at the wood's end. Go half-left over a field to a stile near a gate. Cross the road beyond and go along the track to Bailton's Farm. Go through a gate, cross the farmyard and keep on to bridge the M6 and the railway. Go through a gap stile, cross the field beyond and go over a stile by a solitary oak. Cross a field to a footbridge and gate. Edge the fence on the left, cross a stile and a plank bridge. Cross the next field, aiming to the left of the buildings, to reach two gates. Go through the right-hand gate and continue to Greenhaigh Castle Farm. Turn left along a lane to reach a road. Turn right and, just past the bus station, turn right along a riverside path to return to the start.

REFRESHMENTS:
There are numerous possibilities in Garstang.

Walk 71 KIRKHAM, WESHAM AND WREA GREEN 5¹/₂m (9km)

Maps: OS Landranger 102; Pathfinder 678 and 679.

A walk from the market town of Kirkham to the picturesque village of Wrea Green.

Start: At 436322, the car park, Orders Lane, Kirkham.

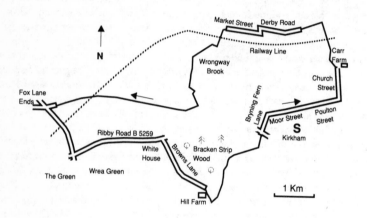

From the car park, in the centre of Kirkham, go to the traffic-lighted junction. Turn right and continue eastwards along Poulton Street, the town's main shopping street, to the Market Square. Turn left into Church Street, pass St Michael's Church on the left, and continue along the track past Carr Farm. Pass under the railway bridge and follow the footpath up a slight rise for some 250 yards. Turn left along the footpath which leads to a built-up area, and go into Derby Road. Go along Derby Road, passing Wesham Hospital, a former workhouse, and cross Station Road into Billington Street East. Turn left into Garstang Road and then immediately right into Market Street. Go along Market Street to the track at the end of it. Take the left fork on to the surfaced track and cross the railway bridge. Turn right and follow the field path to Brook Wood and cross the footbridge over Wrongway Brook. Continue along the field path

136

to the A583. Cross with care and walk a short distance left before turning right into Ribby Road, the B5259. Continue, briefly, along Ribby Road and turn right on to the public footpath that begins just before the entrance gateway to Ribby Hall is reached. Follow this path, crossing over the railway to Fox Lane Ends, the site of an ancient wayside cross. Although the present cross is quite recent, the stone in which it is set is an ancient boundary socket. At the cross turn left and follow Station Road into the village of **Wrea Green**. Turn left at the village green and leave Wrea Green along the Ribby Road. After about $^2/_3$ mile, turn right at the White House into Brown's Lane. Go through Hill Farm before taking the field path on the left which leads over a slight rise to Bracken Strip Wood. Follow the field path along the edge of the wood and cross a small stream. Here the path runs beside an area of marshy grassland which has not been drained or 'improved' for pasture: it is home to a wealth of wild flowers. Grassland areas like this are becoming rare in many districts and the need to conserve them is strong. Continue along the path to the Kirkham by-pass. Cross into Bryning Fern Lane and turn right at the end of it to return to Kirkham town centre via Moor Street.

POINTS OF INTEREST:
Wrea Green – The village is an old Norse settlement that is today one of the most picturesque villages in the Fylde. It is the Fylde's only surviving 'green village', with many charming buildings, such St Nicholas's Church, grouped around the village green.

REFRESHMENTS:
There is a good selection of pubs and cafés in Kirkham, Wesham and Wrea Green.

Walk 72 YEALAND STORRS AND LEIGHTON MOSS 5¹/₂m (9km)

Maps: OS Landranger 97; Pathfinder 636.

Birdlife abounds on this interesting walk.

Start: At 494761, the lane junction, Yealand Storrs.

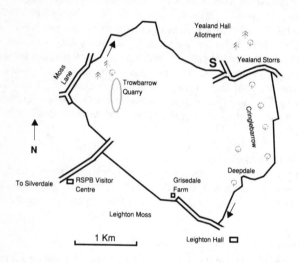

From the junction go eastwards along the lane for almost ¹/₂ mile. Just past its summit, on a bend, go right, along an unsignposted path through a thin wood. Pass an enclosure, and go along a path above the edge of Yealand Redmayne into Cringlebarrow Woods. Edge a clearing, climb into woodland and go left at a junction along a path that goes below the summit. After another path is joined on the left, the path becomes much wider: descend into a clearing and go to the right of two gates, back into woodland. Turn sharp right on approaching a road, and go uphill to a gap near the remains of a summerhouse. Cross a field, go through a wicket and along a beech avenue which overlooks Leighton Hall, on the left. Go through parkland, keeping to the right of a line of electricity poles to reach a surfaced lane near the hall. Turn right, along the lane, passing Home Farm, to reach Grisedale Farm at the lane end. Go through a gate and bear right over a small bridge to reach **Leighton Moss Nature Reserve** at the

Causeway. Take this, crossing the reedbeds. The Causeway passes a public hide just beyond the main dyke from where the local birdlife can be viewed. At the main road, a detour left, of just $1/_4$ mile, will bring you to the RSPB Visitor Centre, but the way is right, along the road for 100 yards. Go left, at a 'Red Bridge Lane' sign. Cross the field ahead, diagonally left, to reach a corner slit stile near a telegraph pole. Maintain the same direction across the next field to reach another slit stile leading to woodland that edges a quarry road. Turn left, along the road, to Moss Lane. Go right for 300 yards. Just past Red Hall Cottages on the left, cross a stile on the right into a field. Follow a path, at first parallel to the lane, then bearing right into woods. Go through a slit stile and continue in the same direction, climbing slightly, to reach a fork in a wall. Go right, over a hill, and descend into a meadow. Cross this close to a wall on you left, past an opening to the Gait Barrows Nature Conservancy Reserve. Continue to a lane and turn right along it. Where it swings left, bear right, through a gate into shrubland. Go through another gate into a bridleway along Yealand Hall Allotment and go back through thin woodland to the Yealands Storrs junction.

POINTS OF INTEREST:
Leighton Moss Nature Reserve – Leighton Moss became an RSPB reserve in 1964 and attracts thousands of twitchers annually. Walking the Causeway could add hours to this super walk.

REFRESHMENTS:
Tearooms at the RSPB reception centre.

Walk 73   **Fairy Steps and Haverbrack**   5½m (9km)

Maps: OS Landranger 97; Pathfinder 627 and 636.

Limestone crags, parkland, woodland and estuary make this walk a joy.

Start: At 489814, Belah Bridge.

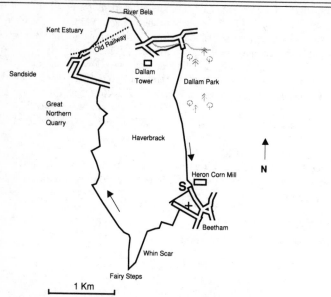

From the south end of Belah Bridge, ¾ mile west of Milnthorpe, turn left along an estate road and left again through a swing gate into Dallam Park. Continue along the Belah to a bridge. Turn right and climb a hillside from where, on the right, Dallam Tower is seen. The route is indistinct in parts, but it is a right of way: go around the side of the next rise to reach a stile in a fence. Cross the field ahead to a slit stile on the left and go through on to a green lane. Follow the green lane to a surfaced lane and go left until just before the first houses in Beetham village. There, turn right, along a path signposted to Hazelslack. Cross a field, enter a wood and turn right along a path that keeps above a wall and curves uphill, passing to the right of a ruined cottage. On reaching a junction go right, uphill. Turn right again on a broad track. Cross another track in a clearing and continue on rising ground and following signs towards Fairy

Steps. A cluster of pines crowns the hilltop, beyond which the path enters a clearing on top of a line of steep crags. Here make a slight detour: from the edge of the crags a narrow cleft zig-zags down. The fissure is a very narrow one and sits on the old coffin road route from Arnside to Beetham. This is Fairy Steps. Go along the top of the crags, the views being better than those from an alternative route along the foot of the scar. On leaving the limestone outcrop the way descends to a wide track. Turn left to a grassy clearing, where the alternative route is met at a signpost. Descend gently through woods to a road. Turn right for 50 yards and follow a signposted route to Haverbrack. The way is straight ahead into woods, keeping on the crest of a hill. Turn right where the path splits, then left at a junction, and right in a few yards. There are lots of other tracks in this wood: ignore them, they are fainter and narrower than your route. Soon a gravel road is reached on top of the huge New Northern Quarry, overlooking Sandside. Go right, following a fence to join a wide track that runs parallel to, but out of sight of, the quarry. Go left to a building, where a brief detour along a path leads to a hilltop and a fantastic view. Return to the building and go along a clear track to the right of it to reach the entrance to a wood where several tracks meet. Go past a wall and immediately go back, left, through a slit stile into a field on top of Haverbrack from where the view north is stunning. Go along the field with a wall on your right, descending sharply and aiming for a signposted stile just to the left of a field corner. Turn left, along a long lane for 150 yards, then right at a 'Sandside' signpost. Cross the road and go down steps to the old railway track. Soon you leave it to go down to the edge of the sands. Go along the sands to the confluence of Belah and Kent, and from there follow the Belah back to the bridge.

POINTS OF INTEREST:
From Haverbrack the stupendous view includes the Kent Estuary, directly below, White Scar and Whitbarrow in the middle distance and Lakeland Fells crowding the northern horizon.

REFRESHMENTS:
There are possibilities in Beetham and Milnthorpe on the route.
The Ship Inn, Sandside, (just off the route).

Walk 74   KELBROOK AND HARDEN CLOUGH   5¹/₂m (9km)

Maps: OS Landranger 103; Pathfinder 670.
One of the most scenic walks in West Craven.
Start: At 903445, Kelbrook church.

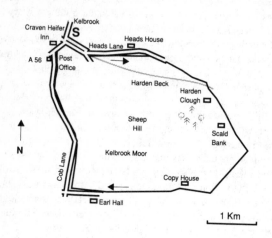

From the church cross Kelbrook Beck and turn left along it, following a tarmac road. Pass Bow Cottage, dated 1853, to reach a bridge. Turn left, across it, on to Harden Road. Turn right, and where it bifurcates, go left along Heads Lane, on to the moor. On approaching Heads House the lane becomes much steeper, but the views are superb. Stay close to a dyke on the left, and after passing a covered-in circular tank on the right, descend to a gate with a stile. Cross into a field with Cocket Farm on your left. Go forward towards a wall, soon seen ahead, keeping to the topside of the field. Go through a metal gate at the end of this facing wall into the next field. Descend diagonally right, passing an old gatepost and aiming for a large tree at the junction of two streams. Cross these at the narrowest point, there being no bridge. Continue along the track, round the back of Harden Clough Farm, and descend towards a shallow, gated ford at the bottom of the farmtrack. A few yards short of it go diagonally right to where a footbridge spans Harden Water near a wall on the right. Cross and descend the clough along a narrow path to cross a stile in a facing wall and continue along a clear track towards Scald Bank Farm. Soon the track begins to climb through moorland and, just short of the farm buildings, goes left, then right, around the back of a barn and up a hill. Keeping a wall on your right, climb the track to a stile in the wall on the right, on to the moor. Go along an undefined track towards a partially walled bridleway seen ahead. Turn right, along it to a stile at a gate where three walls meet. Stay close to the wall on the right as it sweeps round towards distant Copy House to reach two stiles in a facing wall. Cross the left one and go over the pasture ahead, keeping close to the wall on your left because much of the field is very boggy. Soon a wooden seat is reached close to a facing wall. From here take the farm road to Copy House Farm on the right. From Copy House follow a track to the right, along a garden wall, and past a large paddock. Beyond this the track leads to a stile near a gate. Cross and stay close to the wall on our right along an ancient farmtrack which becomes increasingly overgrown. As the overgrowth makes further progress difficult, cross to the left of the track, which now resembles a dyke, where the going is much easier. Continue with the dyke on your right to join an unsurfaced road. Here the area is very marshy and it helps if you cross to the right of the dyke as soon as you are able to do so. Once firmer ground is reached, follow the unsurfaced road to a junction just past the entrance to Earls Hall on the left. Turn right into Cob Lane and go along it towards Waterloo Road. Turn right at the junction and descend into Kelbrook, passing the Post Office, to arrive at your stating point.

POINTS OF INTEREST:
On the descent to Earls Hall the rough marshy areas are compensated for by the beautiful views ahead. Across the valley, on the far side of White Moor Reservoir, Pendle Hill dwarfs Blacko Tower, and gentle slopes of Weets Hill providing contrast.

REFRESHMENTS:
The Craven Heifer Inn, Kelbrook.

Walk 75   **KELBROOK AND BLACK LANE ENDS**   5½m (9km)
Maps: OS Landranger 103; Pathfinder 670.
A fine walk which offers extensive views down the valley towards Colne.
Start: At 903445, Kelbrook Church.

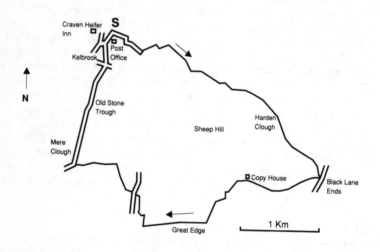

From the Church turn left along Harden Road across the bridge over a stream, and turn left up Dotcliffe Road and left again up a track past a mill. Cross a stile by a cattle grid and turn right, uphill, on the far side of the wall. Turn left at a line of trees and follow them to a gate. Go through, turn right and follow the hedge through two fields. Cross the next field and cross a stile. Turn left along a track to Harden New Hall, go through the farmyard, cross a stile and go over the next two fields. Bear right across the third field and join the Pendle Way, identified by yellow arrows. Cross a stile and go up to harden Clough Farm. Go down the lane past the farmhouse to a stream and bear right over the footbridge. Follow a path uphill to the right. Cross the stile ahead and continue uphill to join the track past Scald Bank Farm. Where the track ends, bear right over a stile. Go diagonally left across the field and turn right at a wall, following it uphill and over a stile to **Black Lane Ends**. At the field corner turn right, following white arrows, up the field to a stile in the wall. Go straight across the next field, over a stile and continue to the far right corner. Go straight over the next field, crossing stiles, and follow the wall to Copy House. Turn left in front of the farmhouse and follow a track through two fields. Turn left, along a wood, and then right over a stile. Cross another stile and bear left to the far corner of a field. Go over the next stile and turn right along the wall at Great Edge. Go straight across the next field, through a squeeze stile and follow a wall downhill. Turn right below the old quarry and follow the stream to a footbridge. Climb the bank and turn right on to a track. Go through a gate to Throstle Nest and immediately turn uphill, then right, along a wall. At a stile, turn left to cross a lane, and go down the enclosed track. Bear slightly right across a field to an avenue of trees. Cross a lane and a stile, go past Oxenards and down to the bridge over **Lancashire Gill**. Turn left and follow the stream to a lane. Turn right and follow Old Stone Trough Lane back to Kelbrook. Turn right at the end of Waterloo Road to reach the church.

POINTS OF INTEREST:

Black Lane Ends – In the 19th century, Black Lane Ends supplied the outlying farms with most of their spiritual and bodily needs: the school, the Methodist's Chapel, the Hare & Hounds!

Lancashire Gill – Marks the old country boundary between Lancashire and Yorkshire. Since 1974 the boundary has run a few miles to the north, transferring our walk from Yorkshire to Lancashire.

REFRESHMENTS:

The Hare & Hounds, Black Lane Ends.
The Craven Heifer, Kelbrook.

Maps: OS Landranger 103; Pathfinder 670.
Pleasant walking through lovely West Craven.
Start: At 906467, the Parish Church, Earby.

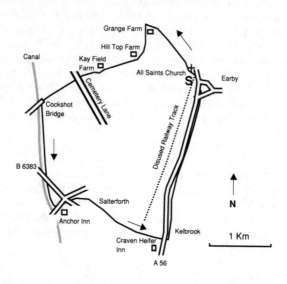

From the Church, go over a stone stile at the rear of the building and take the footpath diagonally right towards the middle of a fence. Cross at a stile partly hidden by holly trees. Go along the path, which first passes in front of, then around the side, of 'The Grange' on the left, and then leads up a hillside to a ridge, and a stile. Cross and stay on the path beside the hedge on your right. Where the hedge ends, go along the ridge, still on the path, following marker stones to eventually reach the top of a little used track. Here, in the corner, to your right, cross a stile, beyond which the path bifurcates. Take the left fork, climbing a small rise. After a lengthy walk across a pasture the path descends to a stile in the middle of a fence. Cross and go forward to another, clearly seen ahead. Beyond this the path goes diagonally across the next field to a stile at the far end. Go over and descend into the next field, continuing towards Kayfield Farm, and passing a cottage. Bear right to reach a farmtrack. Go along it, using stiles, to reach Cemetery Lane. Cross the lane to enter a pasture over a stile. From here there are extensive views of Barnoldswick. Follow the path downhill to cross a small stream near the bottom before turning right and going diagonally across the field ahead towards a gate in the corner. Go through the gate and climb the rise opposite it on to the towpath of the Leeds and Liverpool Canal. Turn left, going under two bridges to enter Salterforth Lane from behind the Anchor Inn. Go along the lane to where the houses end. There, turn left along a clear path to a point just past the entrance to Silent Night Holdings seen on the opposite side of the road (B6383) ahead. Cross the road and descend wooden steps to a stream. Turn right along a clear path, with the stream on your left for most of the way, crossing stiles. The path goes through some settlement beds, crosses a footbridge and another stile. Cross the stream, go over a stile and continue along a fence on your ;left to reach a stile over the fence. Cross and turn right along the fence to reach a concrete ginnel. Go through to a disused railway cutting. Continue along the right-hand of several paths to reach a track. Go on to steps up the opposite side of the cutting. Climb these to enter a pasture and follow the path to a stile into a lane. Go along it and descend alongside the Craven Heifer, on the right. Turn left, along a wide path flanking the A56 back to Earby.

REFRESHMENTS:
The Anchor Inn, Salterforth.
The Craven Heifer, Kelbrook.
The Station Hotel, Earby.

Walk 77　　　　TOCKHOLES　　　　$5^1/_2$m (9km)

Maps: OS Sheets Landranger 103; Pathfinder 689.
A pleasant mix of field, moor and woodland.
Start: At 666215, the car park opposite Tockholes Nature Trail.

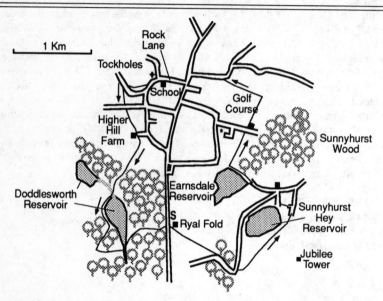

From the car park, near the Royal Arms Hotel, turn left, as waymarked, past the end of Hollinstead Terrace. Go through a kissing gate and go up a track to a gate. Cross a stile beside it and continue through woodland. Where the track descends, ignore the stile ahead and turn sharp left with to reach a stile beside a gate on the right. Go over and turn left (as waymarked by a carving of the Jubilee Tower). Turn right at the next waymarker, climbing along a track. At the top, where the path splits, go left, as waymarked, along a path to reach a stile on to moorland. Go over and turn left along the moorside fence on the left to reach a fork. Bear left, downhill, soon passing Sunnyhurst Hey Reservoir. The path joins a descending, unsurfaced road: continue along this, then go through the smaller of two gates. After 100 yards turn left along a walled lane. Go over a stile and follow a green track across a field. Turn left along a fence, as signed, then, after a few yards, turn right, keep ahead briefly and then bear right to rejoin the original footpath. At a concrete road, turn right, downhill, and at its end turn left along a tarmac road. Where this splits, go right to Earnsdale Reservoir. Cross the dam and a cattle grid, and continue along a concrete track. On reaching a farm, turn left at a millstone, go through a gate and turn right just past a barn.

Go up a field along a wall on the right to reach a stile. Follow the track beyond across a golf course to a point just past a shelter. There, turn left, uphill, along another track and go through a gate. Continue along a wall on the right, crossing two stiles, to reach a gate and gap stile. Do not go over: instead, keep ahead along a bank to reach Coal Pit Lane. Go along it to reach a road. Turn left, then right, along Rock Lane, **Tockholes**. Go past St Stephen's Church and Lodge Farm, then go over a stile on the right and cross a field behind a chapel to reach a stile. Cross the field beyond to another stile. Cross a farmyard to a lane and continue ahead to a stile. Go over and half-left across a field to a corner stile. Follow the fenced track beyond to a lane. Cross, go over a stile and walk uphill along a wall to **Higher Hill Farm**. Cross a signed stile to the south of the farmhouse and follow a wall on the right to a signpost. Climb to a kissing gate into woodland. Turn left. Where the path splits, go right. Cross the dam of Roddlesworth Reservoir and turn left along a path. Cross a stream and curve right to the wood edge. Turn left, back into the wood, soon crossing a stream and going left, towards the reservoir. On reaching a Nature Trail signpost, turn right and climb steeply through woodland to a road. Cross to return to the car park.

POINTS OF INTEREST:

Tockholes – The village takes its name from the Toches Stone, an upright stone that is all that remains of a preaching cross dating from 684AD. The stone is to the left of an arched porch, all that remains of a church dated 1833. A stone, open air pulpit fronts Tockholes School.

Higher Hill Farm – There is a medieval latrine high on the south side of the farmhouse.

REFRESHMENTS:

The Rock Inn, Tockholes.
The Royal Arms Hotel, Ryal Fold.

Walk 78   **WEST BRADFORD AND FOXLEY BANK** $5\frac{1}{2}$m (9km)
Maps: OS Sheets Landranger 103; Pathfinder 669.
The Ribble Way for most of the way, with glorious riverside scenery.
Start: At 743444, the Three Millstones Inn, West Bradford.

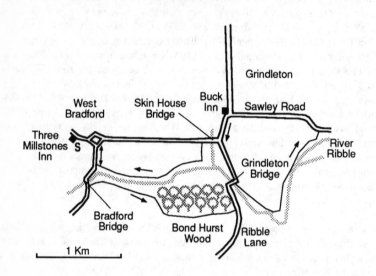

From the Inn turn right, into West Bradford, to reach a road junction. Turn right again, walking through the village and continuing along the road, soon crossing the River Ribble over Bradford Bridge. At once turn left, along the river's south bank, heading upstream to reach a wooded escarpment, Bond Hurst Wood. There, leave the river, turning right, briefly, then left to climb alongside the wood on your left. Cross a field close to its left edge, going over two stiles and turning left into Ribble Lane. Cross the Ribble over Grindleton Bridge and turn right, through a gate signed 'Rathmell Sike'. Now take the stiled path upstream, walking part of the way along the top of a dyke. On approaching a facing fence, bear left to go over a stile in it, then continue upstream briefly to reach a feeder. Turn left, along it, to reach a footbridge. Cross this and the ladder stile ahead. Go uphill across a meadow to the right of a ghyll, continuing straight ahead to join the Sawley road at Foxley Bank. Turn left, along the road, for $^3/_4$ mile to reach Grindleton, passing close to the Buck Inn.

Stay on the road as it bends left and, in a short distance, at a junction, take a right fork over Skin House Bridge. Just past the house beyond the bridge, turn left on a signed, fenced path, to reach the River Ribble. Turn right along the riverbank, soon crossing a gap stile. Follow this pleasant, riverside path, crossing a stile, a bridge over a feeder and a field to reach a concrete bridge over a feeder. Cross and turn left, back to the riverside. At this point, where the river makes a broad sweep to the left, the path keeps to the right of some low ground, staying parallel to a hedge, to reach a stile. This is the only stile, so do not stay with the riverbank.

The path now goes diagonally left, back to the river. Go over a stile under a crab-apple tree and continue to another stile. Stay with the riverside path, soon crossing another stile. Now, as the river curves left, **Bradford Bridge** comes into view and West Bradford can be seen. Cross a stile and a bridge over a feeder, beyond which the path bears slightly right, away from the river, to cross another footbridge over a feeder. The path returns to the riverbank: soon, take a signed path over a stile on the right to reach a road. Turn right, back into West Bradford.

POINTS OF INTEREST:

Bradford Bridge – From Bradford Bridge along the south bank of the Ribble to Grindleton Bridge, then along the river's northern bank, upstream to Foxley Bank this walk follows the Ribble Way. The Way is a middle distance footpath, approximately 70 miles (113 km) long, following the river from its source to where it empties into the sea. It was opened on 1st June 1985, since when it has earned a reputation for the excellence of its scenery and the diversity of its wildlife. The Lancashire section of the route passes through rich farming country, much of which is in private ownership. Along its route there are many picturesque villages, ancient halls and historic buildings.

REFRESHMENTS:
The Three Millstones Inn, West Bradford.
The Buck Inn, Grindleton.

Walk 79   LYTHAM LIFEBOAT STATION   6m (9½km)

Maps: OS Landranger 102; Pathfinder 678.

An easy walk through a landscape of contrasts.

Start: At 367269, the car park beside the Lifeboat Station, Lytham Green.

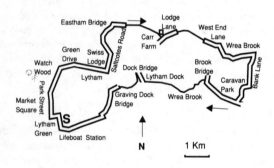

From the car park cross the main sea front road into pebble paved Bath Street and, at the far end of it, go left into Clifton Street. On reaching Market Square turn right into Park Street and continue northwards, going over the railway line and past the entrance to Lytham Hall on the left. At the junction of Ballam Road and Park View Road, go right into the tree-lined avenue known as Green Drive and continue along it to the Swiss Lodge, built in 1884 in memory of one of the Clifton family. Turn left, out of Green Drive, and go northwards along Saltcotes Road. The name here is a memory of times when salt was extracted from sea water in this area. After crossing Eastham Bridge, turn right into the track that leads to Eastham Hall Caravan Park. Do not enter the caravan park: instead, take the wooded path that skirts its southern boundary. Continue along this path, crossing a railway line and pasture land, past the end of

152

Huck Lane farmtrack to reach Lodge Lane. Turn left, eastwards, along Lodge Lane and West End Lane to reach the small village of Wrea Brook. Cross the main A584 road and go eastwards along it. Turn right into Bank Lane and continue southwards, passing a caravan park. At the tidal flats, turn right and continue along the tidal embankment to Brook Bridge. Cross and rejoin the embankment, immediately alongside Wrea Brook. Continue along the embankment until Dock Bridge is reached. Cross the bridge and turn left along the track that passes through the boat building yard. Follow this track through the industrial area to Graving Dock Bridge, named after the process of graving, or cleaning, ship's hulls. Return to the start of the walk via the A584 and the coastline footpath, passing **Lytham Windmill** on the way.

POINTS OF INTEREST:

Lytham Windmill – There has been a windmill at Lytham for the past 800 years. The present one was built in 1805 by Richard Cookson utilising parts from other, disused, Fylde windmills. The shoreline site was chosen to catch local sea breezes. The mill was chiefly used for grinding corn, but a fire in 1918 ended its working life.

Watch Wood and Green Drive are good areas to see many woodland birds, including coal-tit, tree-creeper, greater spotted woodpecker, tawny owl, and chaffinch. These species are augmented in spring and summer by visitors such as willow warbler, chiffchaff, blackcap and spotted flycatcher.

REFRESHMENTS:

There is a wide variety of hotels, pubs, cafés and restaurants in Lytham.

Walk 80 BACUP, SHARNEYFORD AND DEERPLAY 6m (9½km)
Maps: OS Landranger 103; Pathfinder 690.
A walk on the hillsides which give rise to the River Irwell.
Start: At 868230, Bacup town centre.

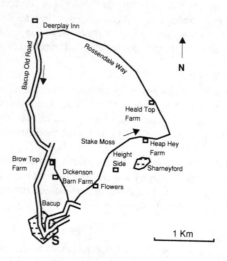

This walk follows a section of the Rossendale Way (marked RW) which can be completed in full by following Walks 55/56, 57/58, 80, 86 and 90/91.

From the town centre – the Hartley of BBC TV's *Juliet Bravo* – cross Yorkshire Street and ascend Lane Head Lane. At the brow of the hill, bear right along Greensnook Lane, by Lane Head Cricket Ground, and continue to the Greensnook Cottages. Take the surfaced, walled lane left, climbing until Christ Church can be seen on the right. Bear left along a surfaced lane past a terrace of cottages and climb to the Flowers Farmhouse. The lane you are on was, until the turn of the 19th century, the main road to Todmorden and Yorkshire. After passing Heap Hey Farm on the left, the lane descends to reach the newer turnpike road at a Toll House. Go left, briefly, leaving the road along a surfaced track and going straight ahead to a crossroads where the Rossendale Way is joined. Go left, along the lower track, towards Heald Top Farm.

Pass the farm on the left and soon cross a stile near a gate. Go through a yard, cross another stile and descend obliquely, staying close to a wall and a fence. Ignoring an obvious left turn, go through the gateway ahead passing, on your left, a large byre and Yew Tree Farm. As it approaches Black Butt the lane does a left and right dogleg through a gate. Continue ahead and, where the track divides at a group of 18th century buildings, continue ahead along a narrow walled lane. Bear left, downhill, and soon turn right and climb past a stone-arched bridge. Once level ground is reached, New Row, once a terrace of worker's cottages, is seen on the right. Cross a stile in a wall opposite and climb a sunken track to a wooden stile. Go over and follow a wire fence to a stone stile at Deerplay Colliery coal depot. Go over, and a few yards on cross the Bacup-Burnley Road. Cross a gated stile in a stone wall and go over the field ahead, leaving over a stile. Continue along a wall to a stile at Height End Farm. Go through the farmyard, leaving over a stile beside a gate on to a surfaced lane, Bacup Old Road. The Deerplay Inn is to the right here. Leave the Rossendale Way by turning left, south, along the ancient saltway. After a mile the lane descends through the remnants of Lane Head Plantation and bears left at Lane Head Farm towards Step Row. Turn right at the main road for 150 yards and cross a footbridge on your left. Climb steeply to Brow Top Farm and turn right into a lane. Go along this past Dickenson Barn Farm and a solitary, strangely out of place arch. Go between high stone walls to where Bacup comes into view once again. Continue straight ahead towards the tower of Christ Church until a surfaced lane is reached. From there retrace your steps downhill, turning right, along Greensnook Lane, past the cricket ground, to reach the town centre.

POINTS OF INTEREST:
Lords Court, on the outskirts of Bacup is the site of the Roebuck Inn, a posthouse on the old packhorse road. Dated 1739, it boasted 'the best bowling green in Lancashire'.

REFRESHMENTS:
The Deerplay Inn.
There are hotels, pubs and cafés in Bacup.

Walk 81 **BARNOLDSWICK AND WEETS HILL** 6m (9½km)

Maps: OS Landranger 103; Pathfinder 670.

An airy, very enjoyable moorland walk with good views.

Start: At 875468, Paddock Laithe Scout HQ, Barnoldswick.

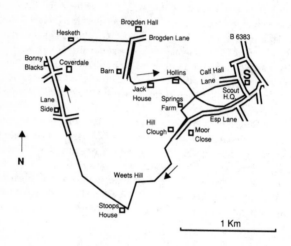

From the Scout HQ, cross the road and go westwards, along Calf Hall Lane. Go through the farmyard of Lower Calf Hill Farm. Go through a metal gate near an outbuilding and along the shoulder of a hill to a gate in a facing fence. Cross the field diagonally towards some trees near a stream and, at the foot of a hill, go along a grassy track to join a wooded lane, reaching Springs Farm through two gates. Cross the farmyard, bearing right to a ginnel leading along the top side of a garage, then beneath some trees to a stile. Descend to cross a stone stile into Esp Lane. Go right, past Moor Close Farm on the left, and Hill Clough Farm on the right, and go through a gate into open pasture. Take a farmtrack until a gate is seen ahead and turn left, off the track, and descend to go through a gate on your left in a corner. Now go uphill, close to a fence on your left, and bear left along the hillside towards some tyre impressions. From here, zig-zag to the hilltop. Continue along a ridge on a path, close to a wall on the left, and cross a stile near the summit. Where the path splits, go right to Weets Hill trig point. Descend the steep end of Weets Hill, aiming for Stoops House Farm, seen on your left. Turn right before the farmyard along a path over moorland to reach a gate in a distant wall, ignoring a minor path branching left to a tile. Go through a gateway and bear right, along a wall, to pass two boundary stones on your left. Go through a gate into Coalpit Lane. Go along it, cross a tarmac road, and pass Lane Side Cottage on the left. Next, on the right, pass the entrance to Coverdale Farm and, a little further on, Bonny Black's Farm on the left. Just beyond the farm, where the road levels beyond a rise, turn right through a gate and take a farm track that bears right to a corner stile. Cross and go in front of a garden, through a wicket gate and over a stream on a bridge. Keeping close to a fence on your right, continue to where a stile in an adjacent wall is seen. Descend to the next field and go diagonally left, uphill, to cross a stile in the bottom right corner. Climb diagonally left to another stile. Cross and turn right through a gate. Go left, along a green lane towards Brogden Hall Farm. On reaching the bottom of the lane, go through one of a pair of gates that leads towards a narrower gate. Beyond this go right to cross a footbridge into a lane that goes past the side of Manor House Farm. The lane continues, eventually sweeping left to pass Jackson House Farm on the right. Go on to a gate with a stile. Beyond, follow the direction of telegraph poles over the next field until, near the top of a rise, the path ahead becomes clear. Go through the yard of Hollins Farm, on the right, and turn left, over a stile beside a gate, to continue along a gravelled track. Go past quarries on your right and later, a path to Cow Pasture Farm on the left. Cross a stream to reach a lane on the opposite side of the hill to Springs Farm. Where the lane used on the outward journey and the one you are now on converge, turn left, along the lower one, to go through a metal gate on the right. Descend along a wooded track to Esp Lane. Go left, descending to Pickles Hippins cobbled footpath and follow it to Town Head. Beyond, take the first left back to the Scout HQ.

POINTS OF INTEREST:
Whenever there is something of national importance to celebrate, beacons are lit on Weets Hill.

The moorland track from Stoops House, northward to Lane Side, was used by carters and packhorses travelling between Colne and Gisburn before the road was built.

REFRESHMENTS:
The Cross Keys, Barnoldswick.
The Seven Stars Hotel, Barnoldswick.
The Fanny Grey, Salterforth.

Walk 82   HOGHTON GORGE CIRCULAR   6m (9½km)

Maps: OS Landranger 103; Pathfinder 689.

A walk along tracks, a canal towpath and through Hoghton Gorge.

Start: At 613266, Hoghton Village Hall Car Park.

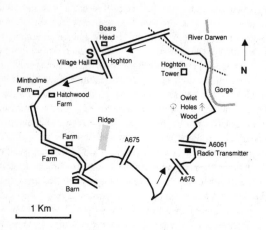

From the car park go right, past Lane Side Farm, and turn right along a track edging Lane Side Cottage. Continue along it, between buildings, to cross a stile beside a gate and to pass tennis courts on your right. Go through a gateway leading to a track lined with tall hedges. Keep straight ahead and go through a gate into a field. Continue along its right edge, and when the path splits take the lower fork. Leave the field over a stile hidden by some bushes to the left of the track, and cross a ditch on a footbridge. Cross the next field close to the hedge on your right and leave it over a corner stile beneath a hedge. Continue along the right-hand side of the next field, leaving over a corner stile with concrete posts. Go across the next field, below Hetchwood Farm, close to the hedge on your right, which soon becomes a fence with concrete posts at the edge of a wood. Climb a stile in an acute corner and go straight ahead along a tree-

158

Walks 84 & 85   RIVERSIDE PARK   6m (9½km) or 12m (19km)

Maps: OS Sheets Landranger 97 and 102; Pathfinder 637, 648 and 659.

A pleasant walk alongside the Lune estuary.
Start: At 445562, Glasson Dock car park.

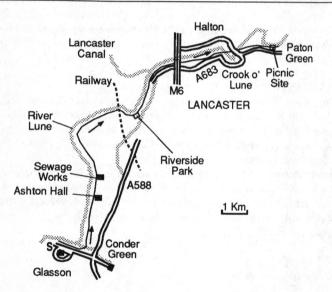

From the car park go eastwards, along the route of the disused Lancaster to Glasson railway between the B5290, on your right, and the Lune estuary, on your left. Cross the River Conder and continue northwards to reach Conder Green picnic area on the site of Conder Green Railway Station where old level crossing posts now mark the car park entrance. The crossing keeper's cottage at Conder Green and the station master's house at Glasson are the only remaining buildings along the line, which is now part of the Lancashire Coastal Way. The whole of this section of the Coastal Way path between Glasson and Marsh Point is a combined footpath and cycle way. Continue northwards, edging the **Lune,** and cutting through Meldham Wood, beyond which are the remains of a wooden platform: the station here was built close to Ashton

lined track. At the end of the track turn left along a lane to reach a junction. Bear right, passing Silcock Farm on the right, then Grimshaw Farm on the left. On reaching a road junction bear right, following a sign to Brindle, and just before a stone barn is reached, close to a sharp right-hand bend, cross a stile on the left, beneath a tree and half hidden by nettles. Continue to the left of a stone post and the remains of a field boundary, cross a footbridge and go along the right-hand side of the field until you pass a pond on your right. There, aim for a stile in a barbed wire fence some 40 yards away. Cross it and continue along the field edge close to the barbed wire fence on the left. Soon the fence becomes a hedge: at the end of the field cross the stile just beyond a stone slab. Continue until a black gate at a ridge is reached. There, go half right towards an open gateway with a detached house in the background. Go to the right of this house and through a gateway on to the B5226. Cross and turn left, passing a house. Go right, over a stile, as signposted, and along a short track to reach another stile into a field. Cross the field close to its right-hand side. At the field end, bear slightly left from the corner, following a thick hedge, to reach a new stile. Cross and go along the right-hand side of a large meadow which has been sub-divided by electric fences, crossing each fence by stile. Keep ahead, crossing a ditch on a stone slab, and follow the fence to the right which leads to a stile on to a canal towpath. Turn left, and soon after going under a bridge that carries the A675 over the canal, take the descending path leading away from the canal to the A6061. In the summer this path is very overgrown. Turn left past the Preston Transmitting Station entrance and, just beyond a detached house, cross the road to reach a track between large stone gateposts. Go along the track until you can see a small lodge near woods on your left. As the track passes beyond the entrance to it, at a hairpin bend to the left, cross a stile on your right and follow a faint track to the River Darwen, descending a slope with Owlet Holes Wood on your left. Turn left close to the river, which is on your right, cross a stile and follow the riverside path through Hoghton Gorge and under the **viaduct** carrying the Preston to Blackburn railway. Beyond the viaduct, cross a footbridge and continue to the ruin of a mill at Hoghton Bottoms. Turn left at the end of the track near the mill and left again between an electricity sub-station and a cottage. Continue along a bridlepath to Long Barn Brow. Cross a stile as the level of the railway is reached and go along the track to Chapel Lane. Turn left, bridge the railway and continue along the lane to the A675. Turn left, uphill, to regain the village hall car park.

POINTS OF INTEREST:
Viaduct – The viaduct, which carries the Preston to Blackburn railway is an impressive example of 19th century engineering.

Walk 83   THE WARLAND RESERVOIRS   6m (9½km)

Maps: OS Sheets Landranger 103 and 109; Outdoor Leisure 21.
Airy walking along the flattest part of the Pennine Way.
Start: At 969178, the White House Inn, on the A58.

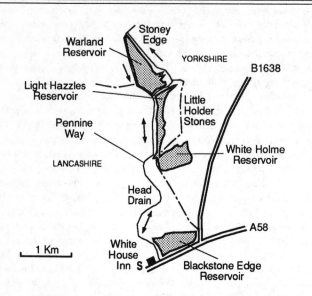

From the Inn, turn left, with care, along the A58, the Rochdale to Halifax road, for a short distance, then turn left again along an Oldham Corporation Waterworks road, following part of the Pennine Way. The road goes along Blackstone Edge Reservoir, on the right. Once past the reservoir, continue along a cinder road with Head Drain running alongside it, on your right, crossing Chetburn Moor.

In little more than 1½ miles Light Hazzles Edge, with its prominent perched boulder, is passed. Just beyond it Light Hazzles Reservoir is reached, on the right. Continue alongside it, staying on the waterworks road to where it bifurcates. Take the right-hand track that hugs Light Hazzles Reservoir on the right. When almost at the head of the reservoir the track curves left and, in so doing, forsakes Lancashire for the West Riding of Yorkshire. Stay on the track for about a mile, and where it ends, continue in a north-westerly direction, with Warland Reservoir close by, on your left.

The way ahead edges closer to the reservoir, passing between it and Sto[...] Edge, on the right. Beyond this the head of the reservoir is reached and the waterwo[...] cinder road is regained. From here a short extension of the walk, north-eastwa[...] along the Pennine Way, reaches **Stoodley Pike**. Turn left, along the cinder track, [...] an embankment, down the western side of the Warland Reservoir. After about ⅔ m[...] the embankment changes direction slightly and it is at this point that the walk [...] enters Lancashire. Soon the southern end of Warland Reservoir is reached and th[...] outward route is rejoined. All that remains now is for the outward footsteps to b[...] retraced.

The terrain is flat and, thanks to the **catchment drains**, dry. So, in both directions[...] the walking is particularly good and, if further spur were needed, the White House[...] Inn awaits at the finish.

POINTS OF INTEREST:
Stoodley Pike – This tower, 120 feet high, is built of natural millstone. The original tower was built in 1814 to commemorate the Peace of Ghent and the abdication of Napoleon. It collapsed and has been restored twice. It commands a fine view of the upper Calder valley, which it dominates. The tower is entered from the north, a dark, forbidding staircase leading to a viewing balcony.
Catchment Drains – The open drains alongside which the Pennine Way passes have been cut into the hillside to allow rainwater from alien watersheds to be fed into the reservoirs. Little Holder Stone, the high ground to the east of Warland and the Light Hazzles reservoirs and to the north of White Holme reservoir is completely surrounded by a contouring drain.

REFRESHMENTS:
The White House Inn, on the A58 at the start.

Hall for the exclusive use of the owner. Continue to reach an old level crossing at the western end of Railway Crossing Lane, which leads eastwards to nearby Aldcliffe. At this point leave the track bed for a path through the saltmarshes of Aldcliffe Marsh, following the Lancaster Coastal Way. This area of saltmarsh attracts large numbers of overwintering and passage birds. This part of the walk is pure joy for ornithologists and binoculars are highly recommended. After about $^3/_4$ mile the path makes a pronounced curve to the right, to match the Lune's course. The river is now no longer separated by marsh: continue to reach Marsh Point, beyond which the way follows Luneside roads, through Lancaster, to Riverside Park, the site of Green Ayre Station.

For anyone wishing to follow the track bed instead of visiting the marshes, simply continue, eventually passing an industrial estate to rejoin the Lune and the Lancaster Coastal Way. Turn right, along the Way to reach Riverside Park.

The longer walk continues upstream along the trackbed of the old Lancaster-Wennington railway. Go past Skerton Weir, which was built over 300 years ago to minimise the risk of tidal salt water flowing upstream, continuing to go under the aqueduct that carries the Lancaster-Kendal canal over the Lune. Continue edging the Lune, soon going under an award-winning modern bridge that carries the M6 over the river. After another $^1/_2$ mile Denny Beck car park is reached. The trackbed continues alongside the river for a further $^1/_2$ mile above Denny Beck, then, where the Lune makes a broad loop, the trackbed continues straight ahead to rejoin and cross the river twice close to Crook o' Lune. Continue past Caton, to the south, and, just past the Bull Beck picnic site, the trackbed brings the walk to a most delightful end. Return, to Glasson Dock, is by Ribble Motor Services omnibus.

POINTS OF INTEREST:
Lune – The Lune Estuary is a haven for bird, animal and plant life. It is a Site of Special Scientific Interest and supports the largest wintering and passage population of wading birds in Britain.

REFRESHMENTS:
The Stork Inn, Conder Green.
There are also plenty of possibilities in Lancaster.

Walk 86   HEALEY DELL TO SHARNEYFORD $6\frac{1}{2}$m ($10\frac{1}{2}$km)

Maps: OS Landranger 109; Pathfinder 690 and 701.

A fine walk around Rossendale Forest.

Start: At 883159, the north end of Middle Healey.

Finish: Sharneyford.

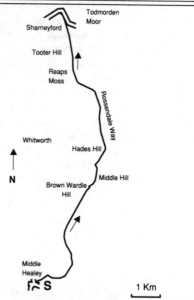

This walk follows a section of the Rossendale Way (marked RW) which can be completed in full by following Walks 55/56, 57/58, 80, 86 and 90/91. This is a moorland walk and proper preparation is recommended.

From the east side of the main road, to the north of Middle Healey, go along Ending Rake Lane to an archway into open country, following a clear track with a wall on the right. Go through a gate into a lane with Hopwood Hall on the left. On reaching a concrete road beyond some cottages, go uphill along a wall, above Hamer Pasture Reservoir, to the site of Brown House. At the end of Brownhouse Wham Reservoir bear left, up a moorland track, climbing past Manstone Edge. At the saddle of Sandy Bed cross a metalled lane and follow a line of boundary stones marked H and S (Hundersfield and Spotland) across common moorland towards Brown Wardle

Hill, standing above **Whitworth**. From the domed summit of Brown Wardle, with its trig point, descend in a north-easterly direction to the saddle, then ascend, bearing right towards the top end of a drystone wall. The path now contours around the right shoulder of Middle Hill for 50 yards and descends gently below spoil heaps. Climb a clough, above the ruins of Higher Hades, to a boundary stone at a wall corner. Continue northwards, along a wall, to where Lancashire Greater Manchester and West Yorkshire meet at a long, triangular enclosure. Cross a wall and follow the enclosure northwards to a walled track. Follow this for $^1/_2$ mile to reach a gate. Go through, along a wall on to open moorland. Follow a fine stone wall along the county boundary for 1 mile, passing a large saddle and a rounded hill, Reaps Moss and Tooter Hill, on the left. Soon a farm track is joined: continue along it to reach a gate. Go pass a brick building and go along a road into Sharneyford.

POINTS OF INTEREST:

Whitworth – 'On a fine Autumn evening, early in October, 1764, a strong, handsome young man with an oaken walking stick bearing a bundle of clothes over his shoulder, walked along the moor at the foot of Brown Wardle towards Whitworth...... he had walked, that day, from Halifax to Walsden'. Taylor settled in Whitworth Square, by the church below, and established the family of doctors, whose fascinating history is told in *The Taylor's of Lancashire, Bonesetters and Doctors, 1750 – 1890* by John L. West.

Walk 87   BLACKO AND FOULRIDGE $6\frac{1}{2}$m ($10\frac{1}{2}$km)

Maps: OS Landranger 103; Pathfinder 670.
A fine mix of field paths, tracks, lakeside and canal walking.
Start: At 860415, Blacko School.

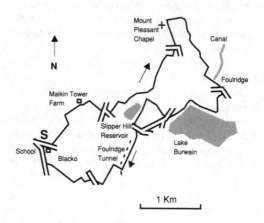

Go along Beverley Road as far as a footpath on the left, signposted 'Blacko Hillside'. Go along this path, over a stile, to reach a hedge under a pylon. Turn left and go towards a farm. Go into the farmyard and turn right, along a lane, to reach a stile in a facing wall. Follow the wall, crossing stiles, into Malkin Tower Farm. Go through a gate and over a stile, beyond which follow a wall downhill. At a stile in the wall, cross and head to the left of a row of cottages to reach another stile on to a road. Turn left, briefly, then right, down a lane as far as a building on the left. Turn left across its front, and cross a stile beyond it. Go along a wall, crossing two stiles and go right, across a field, towards a gate. Follow a path round the corner of Greenshaw Farm's garden and go across the front of the farm to a field corner stile. Go along a track to the back of the farm, and take a track on your left, to a gate with a stile. Go over the field ahead, to cross a stream and then a stile into a lane. Turn left to reach a facing stile. Cross and follow a wall to reach a circular walk sign at a stile. Cross and follow these signs, crossing stiles to reach a road. Continue to a post box. Now turn left, and left again, between houses and bungalows, going downhill through a farm. Go along the road, keeping left, to reach a little gate leading to a path. Pass **Mount Pleasant Methodist Chapel** and turn right along a lane. Opposite a farmhouse, turn right through a gate, cross the field ahead, go over a stile and along a wall on your right. Cross a stile in the field corner, continue over two streams and go over a stile between holly bushes. Cross the bottom of the field, a stile, a road, a field and another stile into a lane. Turn left to reach a stile. Cross the next field, and follow the wall round. Go over a stile on to a road. Go along it to a level open area and take the road ahead. At the end of the road turn right, and continue to the next junction. Go right, up Sycamore Rise, at the end of which a marked path leads to Alma Avenue. Cross and go down a path next to No. 37 to the side of Burwain Lake. Turn right along a path edging the lake, to reach a road. Turn left, then right, past a 'Private Road' sign which applies only to motorists. Go ahead to a stile on the left, opposite a large sycamore. From it a path leads to the bank of Slipper Hill Reservoir. Go left, at a sign, and cross a field to a stile on to a road. Turn left, then right, to the canal towpath at the western end of Foulridge Tunnel. Go along the towpath to bridge No. 145. There, leave the towpath, cross the bridge and go up a lane as far as a stile on the left. Climb a bank, cross a stile and go along a wall on the right. Go over a stile and at a second one turn right, across a field to a road. Cross and go along East Stone Edge Drive to its top. Go to the left of the house to reach steps in a wall leading to a wood. Look for a stile in the wall on your right. Here turn left, along the wall to its end. Turn right along a path. Continue over three more stiles to the road on you right and follow it, left, to a farmhouse. Here leave the road over a stile to the left of a garden and cross a field into a lane. Turn left on to the main road and turn right, briefly, back to the school.

POINTS OF INTEREST:

Mount Pleasant Methodist Chapel – Founded by the Reverend John Barritt, an early convert of John Wesley and one of his itinerate ministers. The chapel and schoolroom were converted from a pair of cottages and opened in 1822.

REFRESHMENTS:

The Rising Sun Inn, Blacko.
The Hole In the Wall Hotel, Foulridge.

Walk 88   TRAWDEN AND COLDWELL   6¹/₂m (10¹/₂km)

Maps: OS Landranger 103; Outdoor Leisure 21.

A walk in the ancient Forest of Trawden.

Start: At 912387, the centre of Trawden.

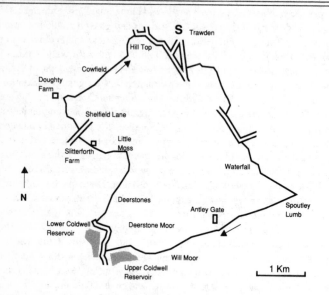

From the Rock Inn, Trawden, walk up the old tram tracks to the right. Just past the first house, turn left, over a stile, and go downhill to the bridge over Trawden Brook. Cross the bridge and a stile, and continue uphill towards Far Wanless Farm. Take the path between the farmhouse and the barn and continue to a track. Where the track turns right, downhill, go straight ahead, over a stile, and cross a field to a small gate. Bear left across the next field to reach a stile beyond the farmhouse. Turn right, down a track, and go left on to a lane. Where this turns sharp left, go straight ahead up the track, round the back of Lodge Moss farmhouse, and through a gate. Follow the wall on your right to the next gate. Cross a field and bear left to a footbridge. Once over the bridge a short diversion, right, along the stream leads to Lumb Spout waterfall. Retrace your steps to the bridge. Now bear slightly left, uphill, towards the far corner of a field. Cross a stile and follow the wall on your right to another stile at the end of the field. Turn right to join the Pendle Way along the foot of Boulsworth Hill. Follow the track for $1\frac{1}{2}$ miles. Near the reservoirs, go through a gate and follow the track to a road. Turn right to reach **Coldwell Inn**. Go right, into the car park, and through a kissing gate behind the Inn. Go straight on, into the field, before bearing left towards a ladder stile. Cross the corner of the next field and continue in the same direction over marshy ground to the wall ahead. Cross over a stream and the wall. Bear diagonally right across a field and go through a gateway in the corner. Veer left across the next field, cross a fence and continue to the far left corner. Cross a stile and go along a wall to a stile. Continue in the same direction across the next two fields to reach a stile where a wall turns a corner. Bear slightly right to a gate, and follow a wall uphill. Go left, round a farmhouse to reach a gate on to a track. Turn left and then right on to a road. After 50 yards, turn left over a stile. Follow the wall on your left to another stile to the field corner. Go over, and then through the middle gateway to turn right along the wall. Climb a stile and follow the wall in the direction of a farm. At the corner of the field, turn right down the valley. Cross the stream by a small alder plantation and continue in the same direction as the stream. Cross a stone stile and go left up a track to Cowfield. Go through the farmyard, then follow the wall on your left. Go through a squeeze stile and along the wall to reach another stile. Take the track which turns right and down the hill. Turn right on to the lane through Hill Top and turn left at the church to return to the start.

POINTS OF INTEREST:

Coldwell Inn – Now a residential holiday and educational centre for handicapped people, the Inn was once notorious for its illegal gambling and cockfighting and was closed in 1939.

REFRESHMENTS:

The Rock Hotel, Trawden.

Walk 89 BRIERFIELD TO WHEATLEY LANE CIRCULAR 7m (11km)
Maps: OS Landranger 103; Pathfinder 681.
This pleasant walk offers some good views of Pendle Hill.
Start: At 855365, the centre of Brierfield.

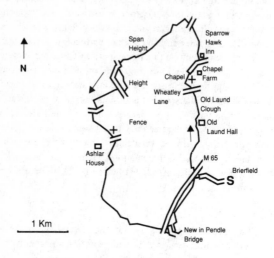

From the centre of Brierfield, go along Railway Street and, before reaching the motorway, branch right, down the old Clitheroe Road. Turn left down a footpath and go under the motorway. Turn left over Quaker Bridge and right along a lane. At the fork, go up the left-hand track through a wood. Cross a cattle grid to Old Laund Hall. Turn left up the track alongside the clough. Go left through the squeeze stile before a gate and follow the field boundary on your right over two fields. Cross the road and continue up the hill. Turn right at the top of the field and go between the cottages. Go through a squeeze stile into the graveyard and past **Wheatley Lane Inghamite Chapel**. Turn left on to the road and right to the Sparrow Hawk Inn. Cross the car park to the stile by the stream and follow the stream uphill, going over two further stiles. Bear right to the far corner of a field, cross a stile and go left over another stile after 20 yards. Follow the stream uphill, bearing slightly right to reach a stile. Beyond, follow the wall on your left. Cross the lane into a field and go straight ahead. Turn left at the top of the ridge. Bear slightly right to a stile, go over and turn right on to a track. Turn left through the gateway before the farmhouse, and bear left across a field to some hawthorns. Go along a ridge, over three stiles, to reach Span Height Farm. Just past the farmhouse go over another stile and bear slightly right to a wall, following it round the corner. Take the path across the field and carry on past Douglass Hall. At the lane, turn immediately left over a stile and cross a field. Beyond the track, bear right towards a sycamore tree. Climb a stile and follow a wall downhill. Cross two stiles and continue along a track to a lane. Turn right, then left in front of Height Cottages. Go through a kissing gate and cross a field to a stile. Go across the next two fields, then over a stile and along a stream. Turn left, through a gateway and cross a field. Turn right on to a lane and after 50 yards go left, down a field. Cross the stream over a stile and follow it downhill to a lane beside St Anne's Church, Fence. Go through the village pub car park and cross a road to a stile. Bear right across a field and cross another stile. Follow the stream downhill over two fields. Cross a ditch and a stile and turn right along a fence, with Ashlar House on the right. At the corner of the field turn left, downhill. Cross a stile in the corner and bear right towards a house. Cross a stile and turn left down a track. Before reaching West Wood End turn left to join the Pendle Way. Cross a clough near a footbridge and follow the field boundary ahead. After $1/_3$ mile cross a footbridge and go downhill to reach a bridge over the motorway. Turn right, over a stile at the end of a path and follow it to New-In-Pendle Bridge. Cross the road and follow a lane, then a path along the river to the bridge crossed on the outward route. Now reverse the outward route to the start.

POINTS OF INTEREST:

Wheatley Lane Inghamite Chapel – The chapel was built in 1750 by followers of the Reverend Benjamin Ingham, a colleague of John Wesley who chose to break with the C of E before the Wesleyans.

REFRESHMENTS:
The Sparrow Hawk, Brierfield.

Walks 90 & 91   STUBBINS TO HEALEY DELL   7m (11km)
or 14$\frac{1}{2}$m (23km)

Maps: OS Landranger 95; Pathfinders 700 and 701.
A fine walk around Rossendale Forest.
Start: At 792182, the Irwell Bridge, Bolton Road, Stubbins.

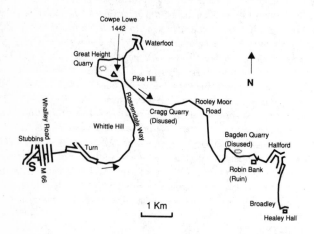

This walk follows a section of the Rossendale Way (marked RW) which can be completed in full by following Walks 55/56, 57/58, 80, 86 and 90/91.

Cross Bolton Road and follow a track to Skeep Hey. Turn right into Leaches Lane to cross the M66. Turn right along Whalley Road. Beyond the first block of buildings, go left up Love Lane. Turn left on to Bury Old Road and in a few yards turn right into Bleakholt Road. Go right again into Rochdale Road. At a restored farm on the left, climb steps and follow a path through a gate. Go sharp left on to a grassy track, which becomes more defined as it crosses open moor. Soon a well-defined track joins from the right, and the way ahead becomes clear. As the summit of Cheesden Valley is reached the path becomes faint, but two gateposts mark the way. The path descends into a valley, crosses a stream and climbs on to open moor, soon crossing a ravine. Where the path splits, bear right. At a track junction, take the left track, cross a meadow and join a tramway. Go along it, skirting disused Great Heights Quarry. Leave the track by bearing right beside Lowe Lodge. Take the path, right, over a boggy area and join a track going uphill. Soon this descends, crosses a pasture and goes past Lowe End. Here, leave the Rossendale Way to walk to Waterfoot: cross a large field and go down a pasture aiming for a courtyard between two buildings. Go through and along a clear route to reach Waterfoot beside the Duke of Buccleugh Hotel. The 7 mile walk ends here. There is a frequent Accrington–Bacup bus service.

Cross the Irwell at Waterfoot Bridge and turn left into Duke Street. Turn left, under an old railway bridge along a steep path which edges woodland and a quarry. Continue to Roughlee, passing to the left of the Manor House and climbing steeply. Cross a stile near the left end of a wall, and continue to the top left corner of a field, where the Rossendale Way is rejoined. Go along a path, aiming for a pile of rubble, and climb the shoulder of Whitaker Pasture, passing an acute bend. Here the well-defined path is left, the way being southerly over open moor towards the left end of a dismantled tramway, where a track crosses it. Take the left section of this track and climb the shoulder of Blackhill. The route now follows a dismantled railway to reach **Cragg Quarry**. Leaving it, go to a junction and turn right to the Rooley Moor Road, soon crossing its summit and descending gradually. Another road joins from the left. When Rooley Moor Road drops into a dip, follow a clear track left. After 300 yards the Rossendale Way branches right and heads towards the tower of a church across the valley. The way is over a stream, past quarry workings and along a ravine top to join a farm road to Robin Bank. Cross a stream on stepping stones and bear right along a climbing, grassy track to a gateway in the Waterworks wall. Go through on to a walled track which turns sharp left to Hellfold village. Fork right on to a footpath which bears right, between buildings, to cross a bridge. Immediately, turn right to the line of a former track. Turn right along the track to Healey and turn left immediately past the viaduct. Descend to a surfaced road and go right to Healey Corner.

POINTS OF INTEREST:
Cragg Quarry – The stone from the Quarry is known as Haslingden Flag. Trafalgar Square is paved with it.

REFRESHMENTS:
The Duckworth Arms.
The Duke of Buccleugh, Waterfoot.
The Royal Hotel, Waterfoot.
The Plane Tree Inn.

Walk 92   GARSTANG AND THE LANCASTER CANAL   7m (11km)

Maps: OS Landranger 102; Pathfinder 668.

An easy walk partly along a canal bank.

Start: At 492449, the riverside car park, Garstang.

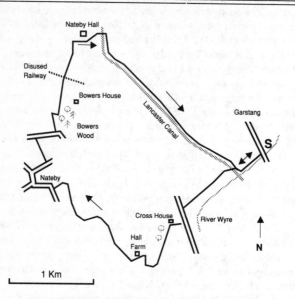

From the car park go right along the riverside path to join a road close to Wyre Bridge.
Turn left across it, then go right, under the arch of the renovated Garstang Corn Mill
and continue alongside the old mill race and the river to go under the aqueduct that
carries the Lancaster Canal over the river. Climb the stairs to the towpath and go left
for 100 yards to reach a stile just short of the canal basin. Go over this stile and cross
the playing field ahead, bearing slightly left to reach a gate in the far fence. Continue
straight ahead across the middle of two fields to regain the riverbank and follow it
until it bends left in the next field. There, keep straight ahead to cross a stile at the
bottom of an embankment. Climb up to the A6. Cross and go left, passing Cross
House Farm on the right, to a gated track signposted 'Kirkland Hall'. Go right, along
this track, passing a farm and Hagg Wood to enter a field. Turn left, close to its left
boundary, leaving through a gate in the corner. Go ahead towards Kirkland Hall to

join an enclosed track at a gate on the right. Go along the track to a junction and turn right to Hall Farm. Go left, along a cobbled road past the front of the farm. When the road bends left go forward through a gate and turn right along another track which, on leaving the field, passes a tip and enters another field. After about 40 yards the track ends at a small bridge over a brook. Go ahead, passing a barn some 50 yards away on the left. Aim for a stile in a fence that goes left where there is a pit on the right. Cross the stile and continue close to the hedge on your right, briefly, around the top of the field, to cross a slab bridge and a stile. Again stay close to the hedge on your right, aiming for a plank bridge and a double stile on the right. Cross the field corner. Continue close to the hedge on your left to re-cross the ditch at another double stile and plank bridge in the field corner. Turn right, close to the hedge on your right, and, when it becomes a fence, bear left to a stile near a gate in a fence close to the field's left corner. Go past a pond, left, and along the left side of the field to Humblescough Lane, reaching it through a gate in the field corner. Go right to Longmoor Lane, Nateby. Leave Nateby, passing a school, a chapel and a post office, and leave the road, right, over a metal gate just past the last house. Continue along an enclosed path to the corner of a triangular field. Cross this along its left side, leaving through a corner gate. Reach Kilcrash Lane over a stile to the right of Hool House. Turn right along the lane, and where it bends right climb a stile on the left signposted 'Winmarleigh Hall'. Go over a footbridge and through a narrow part of Bowers Wood. Now go along a field track, turn left at the field corner before a gateway and continue along the right side of the field to reach the disused Knott End Railway. Cross, go over a stile into a field and eft close to the hedge on your left, passing a copse and ignoring the stile into it. Go straight ahead to a facing hedge and right along it to the field corner to join the farm road to Nateby Hall. Go right, passing a new house that has replaced Nateby Hall, to reach the Lancaster Canal. Go right, along the towpath, to **Rennie's aqueduct** from where you retrace your steps to the car park.

POINTS OF INTEREST:

Rennie's Aqueduct – Garstang's aqueduct was designed in 1793 by Rennie, the same engineer who designed London Bridge and Waterloo Bridge.

Tradition has it that an underground passage, $\frac{1}{2}$ mile long, linked Nateby Hall with Bowers House.

REFRESHMENTS:
Hotels, pubs and cafés in Garstang.

Maps: OS Sheets Landranger 102; Pathfinder 658.
A philanthropist's vision and an ornithologist's delight.
Start: At 340485, the TIC Ferry Landing, Fleetwood.

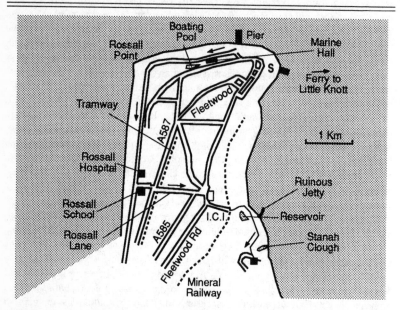

Follow the **Wyre Way** along **Fleetwood** promenade, soon passing the Pier, the swimming centre and the Marine Hall, on the left. Continue past the Marine Gardens and a boating pool, both on your left, then edge the golf links. Now curve to the left with the shoreline and pass **Rossall Point** as the Wyre Way heads south, hugging the shoreline.

When, after about 3½ miles, Rossall School is reached, turn left, along a roadside footpath that edges the school, on the right, to reach the A587. Cross, with care, go over the tram lines and walk ahead along Rossall Lane to reach the A585. Cross, with care, and continue ahead to reach the B5268. Turn right, along the road, passing a caravan site on the left. As the road curves right, turn left, as signposted at the south end of Springfield Terrace. Walk alongside the ICI works on the right, guided by a waymarker to the top of an embankment. Go over a stile, cross a railway line, go over another stile and maintain direction to reach the riverside. Turn right, along a surfaced road, passing a reservoir on the right and a ruinous jetty on the left. Where the road goes into a factory, leave it to continue edging the River Wyre along an unsurfaced track. Follow the track to a road, continuing along it, still close to the river on your left, to reach Stanah Clough. Go over a stile in to Stanah picnic area to finish.

POINTS OF INTEREST:

Wyre Way – The Wyre Way is a 16 mile long walk that explores the history and wildlife of the Wyre estuary and the surrounding countryside from the river's mouth as far upstream as Shard Bridge. This walk covers the first 7 miles of the Way.

Fleetwood – The town owes its existence to the vision of wealthy philanthropist Peter Hesketh-Fleetwood. Before the railway age, the mill workers of Lancashire would have found it impossible to travel more than a few miles and be back the same day, so Hesketh-Fleetwood engaged Decimus Burton, the country's foremost architect, to design an accessible holiday resort for them, and persuaded a railway company to run a line to that part of the coast. Building began in 1836 and the railway was opened in 1840. Hesketh-Fleetwood paid for the construction of many of the early buildings as well as investing heavily in the railway company. To meet his debts he sold off much of his land and eventually went to live in the south of England in poverty.

In the 1830's thousands of day trippers from the mill towns of east Lancashire visited Fleetwood each Sunday and the town grew both as a port and as a holiday centre. With the opening of the Manchester Ship Canal and Preston Docks at the turn of the century, the trade associated with the port went into decline. The fishing industry, however, developed, the town fleet becoming the third largest in the country. The introduction of quotas in the 1970's and rising prices has put an end to most of the commercial fishing, but Fleetwood is still an attractive seaside resort, with much of the charm of its Victorian beginnings still clearly in evidence.

Rossall Point – The length of beach between Fleetwood and Rossall Point provides excellent opportunities for birdwatching. Sea duck such goldeneye and red-breasted mersangers often join the large flocks of mute swans on the boating lakes at Fleetwood and offshore, as many as a thousand eider duck feed over the mussel beds. The beach between the Coastguard Station and Rossall Point regularly supports large flocks of waders, often in internationally important numbers. At high tide the birds often roost very close to the promenade.

REFRESHMENTS:

Farm House Kitchen, Stanah.
There are also numerous possibilities in Fleetwood.

Walk 94   WINMARLEIGH MOSS   7¹/₂m (12km)

Maps: OS Sheets Landranger 102; Pathfinder 668 and 659.

Across Lancashire's only remaining unclaimed mossland.

Start: At 479491, the Patten Arms on the B5272.

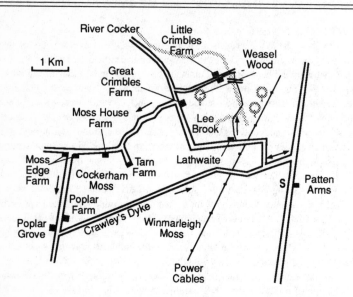

From the Inn, turn right, along the B5272, northwards towards Cockerham and, in a short distance, turn left, along a lane. Cross a facing stile beside a gate and continue down the lane until a gated lane is reached on the right. Turn right along this to reach Langthwaite Farm. Just past the building on your right, turn right, through the farmyard to reach a gate beside a garden wall. Follow the track beyond through a gate and then stay close to a hedge on the right to go through another. Stay close to a hedge on the left, ignoring a gate in it to reach the field corner. Turn right beside a fenced dyke, Lee Brook, soon crossing a stile beside a gate and a footbridge in the next corner. Cross a field and go over the River Cocker on gated Burns Bridge. Turn left, through a gate, and go along the riverbank to another gate. Cross a field and go over a stile close to a bridge that gives access to Little Crimbles Farm. Do not cross the bridge: instead, continue downstream with the river still on your left. Soon you reach and cross a

178

footbridge. Now go over a stile and turn half-left across a paddock to reach a gate between out-buildings. Go through and turn right to cross the farmyard. Follow a track to the farm road, turning along it, passing Weasel Wood on the left, to reach a T-junction. Turn left along a road to reach Great Crimbles Farm, on the left. Here, turn right along Gulf Lane, passing Tarn Farm and Moss House Farm, both on the left, to reach Moss Edge Farm.

Turn left between a barn and the Granary Farm holiday cottage, following a lane to pass Poplar Farm, on the left, and Poplar Grove, on the right. Soon after passing Poplar Grove a gate with an adjacent stile is reached on the left: cross the stile and walk beside a moss boundary, on the left, to cross a footbridge. Keep ahead, staying as close as you can to Crawley's Dyke, on the left, which cuts across **Winmarleigh Moss**. After almost $1\frac{1}{2}$ miles, cross a footbridge into a field and continue beside the dyke to cross another footbridge. Stay beside the dyke, soon crossing a stile on a bridge just before power cables cross the walk. Continue along the dyke crossing a stile to reach an enclosed track, Thorough Way. Follow this to reach the outward leg at the turn to Langthwaite Farm. Now retrace your steps back to the start.

POINTS OF INTEREST:

Winmarleigh Moss – The mosses across which this walk passes are composed of lowland peat which at one time spread across most of the Lancashire Fylde. The place is of particular interest to naturalists because of the fauna and the insect life to be found there and has been designated an area of special interest.

At the time of the Norman Conquest few people lived on the mossland, most of which was uninhabitable. Not until the 12th century did draining begin. Very slowly the mosslands were claimed as meadows, or brought under the plough.

Farming the mossland was a hard life and poverty was widespread. The dwellings of both freeholders and copyholders were little more than hovels and not until the latter part of Queen Victoria's reign was there any real sign of improvement.

The draining of the mossland has been a continual struggle with nature that even today has not been won. It is to be hoped that it never will be, because what is a hostile environment to humans provides sanctuary to other forms of life.

REFRESHMENTS:

The Patten Arms, on the B5272, at the start.

Maps: OS Sheets Landranger 97; Pathfinder 637.

A pleasant walk along a canal towpath, by the riverside, over open moorland and down pleasant lanes.

Start: At 525730, the parking area in the lane near the canal bridge, Borwick.

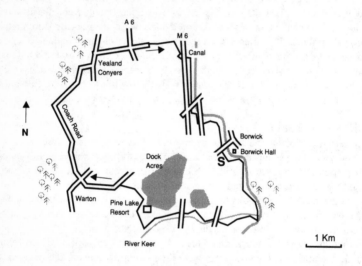

From the parking area go on to the towpath and follow the canal as it meanders south, towards Capernwray, passing, on the opposite bank, a wooded area. Just past a railway bridge the canal crosses the River Keer on an aqueduct at Keer Bridge. At the next bridge leave the canal and go along a path for 50 yards to where it splits. Go over a facing stile into a field. Cross diagonally right, go under a railway bridge, and reach a footbridge beside the River Keer. Go along the riverbank to a lane. Turn right, over the river, and go left along the opposite bank and under the M6 on a catwalk. Beyond, the path skirts Dock Acres, large flooded gravel pits, and passes Pine Lake Resort along a gravel path, close to a road on the left. Take a green path, parallel to, then reaching the A6. Cross, with care, and go along a green lane, under a railway arch.

Continue between tall hedges to join a lane into Warton village. Turn left along the main street, then right at the Black Bull and up a rise into a car park below a quarry. Leave the quarry floor through a wall, and turn right at a junction of paths. Go on to another junction and continue directly ahead, along a level track edging the top side of a meadow. Go along the edge of a wood, keeping right at every junction of paths and keeping the wall on your right. Cross two acres of bracken, and continue into dense woodland. Go left to join Occupation Road, a broad bridle track, and stay on it to reach the Coach Road, a surfaced lane. Go left for $^1/_2$ mile, to reach a footpath on the right, signposted 'Yealand Conyers'. Go along this path, past a lime kiln and between clumps of trees. Just before a wall, fork left through bushes, with the wall on your right, to reach a tarmac road. Turn right into Yealand Conyers. Turn left at a junction of lanes, then right, along another, to the A6. Cross, with care, and take the farm lane opposite into fields. Keeping to the wall side, descend towards the motorway, circle right and take the passage under it to join the canal towpath. Turn right to the once famous Tewitfield Locks, which now, with no lock gates, have become a series of small waterfalls. Continue past a marina and stay with the snaking canal, past bends and under bridges, to where the walk began at **Borwick**.

POINTS OF INTEREST:
Borwick – Borwick Hall, with its imposing pele tower, dates from the 13th or 14th century. It now belongs to the Lancashire Youth Clubs Association.

REFRESHMENTS:
The Black Bull, Warton.

Walk 96 GREENBER FIELD AND BARNOLDSWICK 9m (14½km)

Maps: OS Sheets Landranger 103; Pathfinder 670.

This walk crosses a distinctive limestone landscape moulded during the Ice Age.

Start: At 885485, Greenber Field Locks.

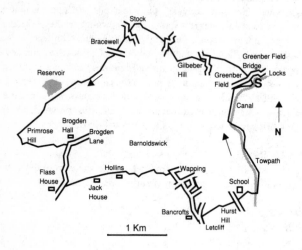

From the locks, leave the canal along the path next to the pump house. Turn left on to the lower road, and after 100 yards turn right into a farmyard. Go through it to reach a track. After ½ mile, turn left off the track to reach a stream, and follow it to a gate. Go through and continue to a bridge. Go over the bridge and continue in the same direction, passing **Gilbeber Hill** to reach a stile to the left of a ruined barn. Go over and uphill to reach a fence. Turn right towards the bridge over Stock Beck. Cross it and follow the field boundary uphill, bearing left on approaching farm buildings. Cross a wall stile to reach Stock, go down to a track and turn left. Pass between a house and a barn, go through a gate and follow a sunken track to the left. Keep straight on, downhill, in the direction of the bridge over Stock Beck. Cross and go ahead to reach and cross a stile. Now follow a hedge on the left side of a field to reach the road at Bracewell. Turn right, and take the second left, towards Priory Cottage. After a few yards turn right, through a gate. Pass to the right of a tennis court, and cross a stream to reach a stile in a wall. Skirt to the left of a plantation on the hill and continue in the same direction to a fence. Turn right along it and, just before the end, cross the field to its right-hand corner. Cross a stile, turn left and follow the wall past a reservoir. Go through a gate and continue along the field boundary. At the top of the hill turn left, through a gate, and immediately go right over a stile into a field. Go downhill, cross a track and go over the stile to the right of a farmhouse. Go through a gate and cross a bridge. Turn left along a stream, then go right to a wall stile. Cross and go up the side of a field, then down to a stream. Cross a bridge and continue along the field boundary. Turn right, across the field corner, then left, along a fence. Go through a gate and follow a track downhill. Turn right, over a bridge and go along a lane to the left to reach Brogden Lane. Go right along this for $^1/_2$ mile. Just past a barn, turn left over a stile. Bear slightly left across a field to a wall stile. Go over and descend to a track. Turn right and follow the track past two houses and over a stile. Continue along a wall to reach a gate next to a line of trees. Go across the next field in the same direction towards Hollins. Go through a gateway and skirt the house garden. Turn right, over a stile, in the farm corner and go through a gate. Turn left, down a lane, and after 300 yards turn left over a stile into a field. Veer slightly left and cross the field, going through a squeeze stile. Bear right where the hedge turns a corner, and turn right down a track. Just past a cattle grid go right, down an enclosed path. Turn left on to Esp Lane, then left into Westgate. Turn right before the car park opposite John Street, and follow the path past a sawmill. Turn right up Forty Steps to reach the Colne Road opposite Bancroft Mill. Turn left, up the hill, then right into Manchester Road. After about 150 yards, go left into a lane leading to Letcliffe Park. At the lane end, walk on, bearing right to reach a wall stile. Go over, turn right and continue for 150 yards to turn left on to a track which descends to the B6383. Turn left, then right, into a lane in front of a school. After 200 yards take a path that forks right from the lane and continue to reach the Leeds and Liverpool Canal. Cross the bridge and turn left on to the towpath. After $^1/_2$ mile cross the road bridge to the opposite side and continue back to Greenber Field Locks.

POINTS OF INTEREST:

Gilbeber Hill – The hill is reputedly the spot where Prince Rupert's men camped while marching through West Craven during the Civil War.

REFRESHMENTS:

Numerous pubs and cafés in Barnoldswick.

Walk 97   **BARROWFORD AND SLIPPER HILL**   9m (14¹/₂km)
Maps: OS Sheets Landranger 103; Pathfinder 670.
*A watery theme with riverside walking, reservoirs and a canal
towpath to finish.*
Start: At 863401, Pendle Heritage Centre, Barrowford.

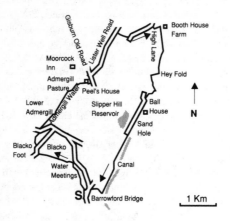

Leave the car park and follow the river to a road. Go left over the bridge and
immediately right by a mill. Follow the road past the last house on the right where a
track goes along the river to Water Meetings. Turn right, over the bridge and
immediately go left. Follow the track to the right and cross a footbridge. Bear right
over a field to reach a stile on the skyline. Go straight over the next stile to reach
another stile on the skyline. Go straight over the next stile to reach another stile and
go past Blacko Foot to a road. Turn right to just past a bridge. Turn left along the river
crossing two stiles and emerging through a small wood to a lane. Go left over a bridge,
then right, to cross a stream. Walk for 300 yards, then go uphill to a stile. Cross two
fields and then a stile into the grounds of a house at Lower Admergill. Go to the right
of the house to a lane. Turn left, going ahead, over a stile, where the lane bends. Cross

two fields, bearing right to a stile and crossing a stone bridge. Climb a hill, bearing left near the top to reach the Gisburn Road. Cross the road to a stile on the left, then go diagonally left, and follow a wall to an iron gate. Keep a farm to your left and cross a stone stile ahead. Follow a track to the top, cross the next field and turn right, then immediately left down an enclosed track. Turn left on to Gisburn Old Road. After 200 yards turn right through a kissing gate. Follow the wall on your left to another kissing gate, then go along Lister Well Road for $^2/_3$ mile. Where the track falls away, downhill, turn right over a stone stile. Cross the field ahead on a path, and cross the next field to a stile in the left corner. Follow an enclosed track to a road. Turn right and after 100 yards go left into a field. Go towards a farmhouse and turn right in front of a wall. Where the wall turns left, go straight across a field to a stile. Go over and along a path, bearing left towards a wall and going right alongside it. Cross a track and two narrow fields. Cross County Brook on a footbridge and immediately turn right to a lane. Turn right, along it, for $^1/_2$ mile, towards Mount Pleasant Chapel (see Note to Walk 87). Turn left over a stile just before the chapel and cross a field. Follow the track to a road junction. Turn right on to a road and, after 25 yards, turn left into a field. Bear right, across the field, go over a stile and turn left towards a farmyard. Go right, over a stile, cross the drive, go over another stile and follow the wall round to the left, over two fields and on to a track. Go downhill, past Ball House. At the track's end, cross the corner of a field to a stile. Follow the enclosed path past Sand Hole and continue to the path around Slipper Hill Reservoir. At the corner of the reservoir take the path to the left. Follow the path, bearing right to a stile. Turn left on to a lane, then go right to a path. Go over a bridge, then go left over a tunnel entrance. Turn down to the left bank of the Leeds and Liverpool Canal and follow the towpath. At the fifth lock turn right, over a stile, onto the old road bridge. Go along a wide track into Bolne Road, and turn left to the Heritage Centre.

REFRESHMENTS:
Available at Barrowford and Foulridge.
The Moorcock Inn.

Walk 98   **RIBCHESTER AND STONYHURST**   9m (14¹/₂km)
Maps: OS Sheets Landranger 103; Pathfinder 680.
A walk along the Ribble.
Start: At 664356, Ribchester Bridge.

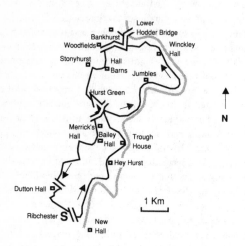

From the north end of the bridge go right, following Ribble Way signs along a track
to Dewhurst House. Turn right into a farmyard and follow Ribble Way signs to the
riverside, passing Hey Hurst and Trough House. Turn left, along a lane to Hurst Green
and take the path on the left side of the Shireburn Arms down to the river. Follow
Ribble Way signs past Jumbles, ancient burial mounds, and Winckley Hall to reach
Lower Hodder Bridge. Walk up the road and go through a gate on the right. Go
diagonally right, uphill, and through a hedge at its corner to continue over a stile in a
fence into the garden of Bankhurst. Turn left and go down the lane to a road. Turn
right and go left down the first lane on the left to pass Hall Barns Observatories and to
reach the front of **Stonyhurst College**. Go down the driveway to the College gates.
The Almshouses are on the left. Continue along a track, curving left, to reach Hurst

Green. Take the Longridge Road to reach the Parish Church and turn left there on to the farm road down to Merrick's Hall. Go through the farmyard into a field and cross it towards the tree line to reach a point where a building is seen through the trees. Now go through a gate to the right of a corrugated iron hut. Go through a gate, cross a footbridge and go up to Bailey Hall. Go along a farm lane, over a cattle grid and past a henhouse in a field to the right, to reach a lone tree on the right of the road. Continue for 80 yards and then bear left, off the road, and go forward to what looks like a stile in a fence. Cross a footbridge and go over the next field, bearing left to cross a stile on the edge of a wood. Descend a shallow valley, cross a footbridge and go along a farm road to Grindlestone House. Go through the farmyard and over a stile. Follow the fence on your right, crossing three stiles, to reach a road. Go left to Dutton Hall. Go to the front of the hall and through a gate on the left. Turn right and go towards a large, blue tank. Keeping the tank on your left, cross a large pipe to the left of a field wall. Follow the wall to go over a stile, and walk down to a stream. Continue downstream to cross a footbridge. Go ahead, over a stile, and follow the fence on your left to reach a gate with a double stile. Continue over stiles, going downhill, between two old ponds, to cross a stile by a gate. Take a sheep track down and over a footbridge. Turn left and walk to a fence stile. Cross and go left, over the next stile, and continue to reach a road over a hedge stile to the left of a gate. Walk down to Lower Dutton. Walk ahead, then go left over stile beyond the farm. Go across a field and cross a stile on to a riverbank. Turn right and walk back to Ribchester Bridge.

POINTS OF INTEREST:

Stonyhurst College – Without doubt, the most prominent house in the Ribble Valley is Stonyhurst. It was the main residence of the Shireburn family until 1794, when it was placed at the disposal of the Jesuit Fathers of Liege. Today it is one of the finest Roman Catholic Boarding Schools for boys in the country.

REFRESHMENTS:
The Bailey Arms, Hurst Green.
The Shireburn Arms, Hurst Green.

Walk 99 RIBCHESTER AND BOLTON FOLD CROSS 9m (14¹/₂km)

Maps: OS Sheets Landranger 103; Pathfinder 680.

A walk that includes a section of the Roman road from Ribchester to the small supply fort at Kirkham.

Start: At 650351, the Roman Museum, Ribchester.

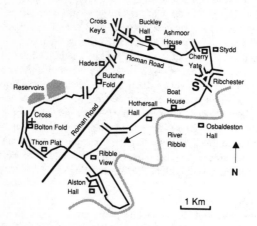

From the Museum follow the Ribble Way west, past the Boat House to Hothersall Hall. Go along a lane, past Hothersall Lodge, up the hill and left at Greenacres. Walk along the line of the Roman road and go through a gateway on to a track. Turn left, go down to Brook Hall and turn right to the riverbank. Follow the riverside path around a bend in the river to Boot Farm. Beyond the farm, turn left to Alston Hall. Return up the track from Brook Hall to a gateway and continue through a farmyard into a farm lane. Go right to Jinkinson's farm track and turn left along it to a farm road. Go left and walk down to the road. Go right to the main road and go along it to the first lane on the right. Bolton Fold Cross is in a field to your right. Go along a lane by the side of the reservoir, going right where it forks, through a kissing gate. Follow the hedge on your left, cross a stile and pass a pond. Now follow the fence on your right, around a corner to reach, and follow, firstly a fence then a hedge, to reach a footbridge. Cross and go up a bank and across a field, keeping in the hollow on your left. Cross a footbridge and go up to a stile on to a road. Go up the lane opposite and cross a stile in a fence. Go along a hedge on your left, cross a stile on your left and follow another fence on your left to reach a stile into Butcher Fold. Enter the farmyard and, following yellow arrows, leave through a metal gate. Follow the hedge on your left and cross a corner stile. Cross the field ahead, leaving over a stile and continuing to some trees. Cross a stile and take the path to Hades Farm. Walk to a road. Go right, then left into Lord's Farm. Go through the farmyard by the side of a barn, and through a gate on the left. Follow a mix of fence and hedge on your right and go through a second gateway, on your left. Follow the fence on your left and cross a stile. Go over another stile and continue, with a hedge on your left, to go through a gate at Buckley Gate. Go down the road, bear left and go down the first farm track to Buckley Hall. Go in front of the Hall, and through a field gate. Cross a field to its far, bottom corner and cross a stile into a wood. Go on to reach, and cross, a footbridge and then follow the stream down to go over another footbridge. Go diagonally right, uphill, to follow a fence on the right to reach a gate to Ashmoor House. Go past the front of the House and along a lane to Boyce's Farm. Pass a barn and go left through a gate. Go past a pond and over a footbridge. Follow the fence on your right to Cherry Yate. Go up the road, then right, over a stile at the end of a garden. Go diagonally right, downhill, through a gate and on to enter a farmyard through a gate. Continue to Stydd Church. Go past Shireburn Almshouses to reach Stonebridge and turn right there, back into **Ribchester**.

POINTS OF INTEREST:
Ribchester – The Ribchester ferry, which ran between Osbaldeston Hall and below Ribchester, is first mentioned in 1355, when Adam Bibby of Ribchester, granted William-de-Braddeley, *fferiman*, the right to carry people across the Ribble.

REFRESHMENTS:
The White Bull, Ribchester.
There are also numerous other possibilities in Ribchester.

Walk 100   BLACKPOOL'S GOLDEN MILE   12m (19km)

Maps: OS Sheets Landranger 102; Pathfinder 678 and 658.

At night, during the Illuminations, this is Lancashire's most brilliant walk.

Start: At 336485, the tram terminus, Fleetwood.

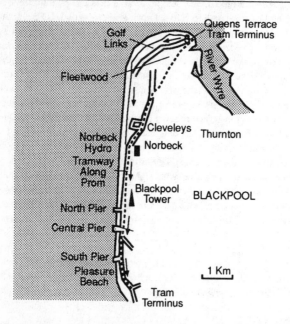

From the terminus at Queen's Terrace, **Fleetwood**, go left, following the route of the Lancashire Coastal Way, along the promenade, passing Fleetwood pier and the Marine Hall on your left. Continue past the Marine Gardens, also on your left, and a golf course, bearing left with the shoreline to pass Rossall Scar, on the right, as the Coastal Way heads south, guided by Blackpool Tower and the new Roller Coaster. After about a mile, just past a car park, **Cleveleys** is reached: to your right now a succession of breakwaters is passed. Go past Cleveleys Jubilee Gardens and a clock tower, and ½ mile further on, Blackpool's famous tramway meets the promenade, staying with it to the end of the walk.